3

PATHWAYS

SECOND EDITION

Reading, Writing, and Critical Thinking

Teacher's Guide

COLLEEN SHEILS

NATIONAL GEOGRAPHIC
LEARNING

Australia • Brazil • Mexico • Singapore • United Kingdom • United States

NATIONAL GEOGRAPHIC
LEARNING

Pathways Teacher's Guide 3,
Reading, Writing, and Critical Thinking,
Second Edition

Colleen Sheils

Publisher: Andrew Robinson

Executive Editor: Sean Bermingham

Development Editor: Melissa Pang

Director of Global Marketing: Ian Martin

Product Marketing Manager: Tracy Bailie

Media Researcher: Leila Hishmeh

Senior IP Analyst: Alexandra Ricciardi

IP Project Manager: Carissa Poweleit

Senior Director of Production: Michael Burggren

Senior Production Controller: Tan Jin Hock

Manufacturing Planner: Mary Beth Hennebury

Art Director: Brenda Carmichael

Compositor: MPS North America LLC

Cover Photo: A rock moves across the Racetrack Playa in California's Death Valley National Park: © KiskaMedia/iStock/Getty Images

For product information and technology assistance, contact us at
Cengage Learning Customer & Sales Support, cengage.com/contact

For permission to use material from this text or product,
submit all requests online at **cengage.com/permissions**
Further permissions questions can be emailed to
permissionrequest@cengage.com

ISBN-13: 978-1-337-62485-5

National Geographic Learning
20 Channel Center Street
Boston, MA 02210
USA

National Geographic Learning, a Cengage Learning Company, has a mission to bring the world to the classroom and the classroom to life. With our English language programs, students learn about their world by experiencing it. Through our partnerships with National Geographic and TED Talks, they develop the language and skills they need to be successful global citizens and leaders.

Locate your local office at **international.cengage.com/region**

Visit National Geographic Learning online at **NGL.Cengage.com/ELT**
Visit our corporate website at **www.cengage.com**

Printed in the United States of America

Print Number: 01   Print Year: 2018

CONTENTS

TEACHING WITH *PATHWAYS*

In *Pathways*, real-world content from *National Geographic* publications provides a context for meaningful language acquisition. Each unit's high-interest content is designed to motivate both students and teachers alike. Students will learn essential vocabulary, review important grammatical structures, and practice reading and writing skills that will allow them to succeed in academic settings.

The features in each unit of *Pathways Reading, Writing, and Critical Thinking* include:

- *Academic Skills* listing at the start of each unit that highlights the unit objectives
- *Explore the Theme* pages that introduce the unit theme and key vocabulary
- Authentic readings that present target vocabulary and provide ideas for writing
- Audio recordings of all the reading passages
- *Grammar References* that present key structures and language for writing assignments
- *Vocabulary Extension* exercises that can be used in class or for self-study and review

The *Pathways* series is designed to be used in a wide variety of language-learning programs, from high schools and community colleges, to private language institutes and intensive English programs. Pacing guides for implementing the program in various teaching situations are provided on page xii.

Teaching Academic Literacy

In addition to teaching essential English language reading and writing skills, the *Pathways* series promotes other aspects of academic literacy that will help students succeed in an academic setting, such as:

- Visual literacy
- Critical thinking
- Classroom participation and collaboration skills
- The ability to use technology for learning

Students build essential academic literacy skills while encountering stories about real people and places around the world. The use of high-interest content from *National Geographic* publications builds global and cultural awareness, and develops learners' understanding of important 21st century issues that affect us all.

Increasing Visual Literacy

In this digital age, the ability to process photographs, maps, charts, and graphs is essential. Most academic journals—both online and in print—present information with some kind of visual aid. Similarly, *Pathways* uses high quality infographics and photographs to help students develop the ability to interpret and discuss visual information.

STIMULATING INFOGRAPHICS from National Geographic publications help explain complex processes.

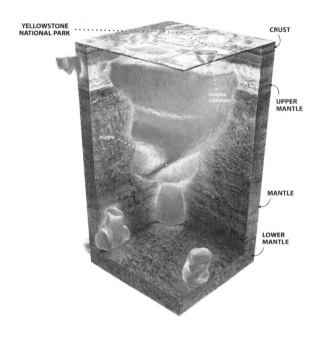

CHARTS, GRAPHS, AND TIMELINES present information visually.

Growing Urbanization

Percentage of population living in urban areas of more than 300,000 people, 1950–2050

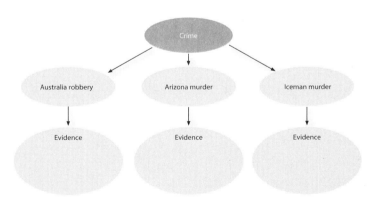

MAPS show locations and geographical features, and illustrate historical facts and current trends.

GRAPHIC ORGANIZERS show the relationships between ideas in a visual way.

Using Videos

Pathways uses videos from National Geographic's award-winning film collection. The videos present a visually dynamic perspective of each unit's theme. Each video's narration has been carefully graded to match student proficiency levels.

Teaching Video Viewing Skills

Pathways promotes visual and digital literacy so learners can competently use a wide range of modern media. Videos differ from reading texts in important ways. Because students are processing more than just words, extra layers of meaning need to be understood:

- Information about the video's setting
- Signs and captions identifying people or places
- Maps and diagrams explaining information and processes
- Nonverbal communication such as facial expressions, gestures, and body language
- Music and sound effects

The transcripts for the videos can be found in the Teacher's Guide on pages 117–122.

The Video Section

Each unit features activities for students to do before, while, and after watching the video.

BEFORE VIEWING

This section provides background knowledge and stimulates interest in the topic by:

- predicting video content using images and captions.
- providing a short reading passage that includes background information about the topic.
- pre-teaching vocabulary from the video.

WHILE VIEWING

As they watch the video, students focus on:

- checking their predictions.
- identifying main ideas.
- watching and listening for particular details.
- inferring opinions and attitudes.

AFTER VIEWING

Students check their comprehension and relate the video to other aspects of the unit by:

- applying the ideas in the videos to their own lives and communities.
- synthesizing information from the video and information from the reading passages.

Building Critical Thinking Skills

Students today are expected to do more than just learn and memorize information. The ability to think critically about a topic—to analyze, evaluate, and apply ideas—is increasingly essential in an academic setting. *Pathways* actively fosters critical thinking while students read, listen, write, and discuss.

Critical Thinking and Language

Critical thinking requires a deep processing of language, which aids language acquisition. Articulating complex responses requires creative thought and word associations, which lead to better comprehension and retention of target language.

These are some of the critical thinking skills covered in *Pathways*:

- **Analyzing** Examining a text in close detail in order to identify key points, similarities, and differences.
- **Applying** Deciding how ideas or information might be relevant in a different context e.g., applying possible solutions to problems.
- **Evaluating** Using evidence to decide how relevant, important, or useful something is. This involves, for example, looking carefully at the sources of information, or the reasons the writer provides for or against something.
- **Inferring** "Reading between the lines;" in other words, identifying what a writer is saying indirectly, or implicitly, rather than directly, or explicitly.
- **Synthesizing** Gathering appropriate information and ideas from more than one source and making a judgment, summary, or conclusion based on the evidence.
- **Reflecting** Relating ideas and information in a text to your own personal experience and viewpoints, and forming your own opinion.

Each unit contains several opportunities for critical thinking. There is also an expanded *Critical Thinking* task in one of the *Understanding the Reading* sections:

CRITICAL THINKING   As you read, look for words and phrases that help you **analyze levels of certainty** about information in the passage.

Words that indicate the information is factual or certain:
definitely, know, prove, clearly, show, and *this means*

Words that indicate the information is mostly certain:
believe, probably, suggest that, argue that, and *likely/unlikely*

Words that indicate the information is not certain:
possibly, could, might, perhaps, and *maybe*

D   Read these sentences from "A Body in the Mountains." How certain is the writer about each underlined piece of information? Rate them (3 = very certain; 2 = mostly certain; 1 = not certain). Then share the reasons for your answers with a partner.

CRITICAL THINKING:
ANALYZING
CERTAINTY

1. _____   Scientists believe <u>he lived about 5,300 years ago in an area north of what is now Bolzano, Italy</u>.

2. _____   Wounds on the Iceman's body clearly show that <u>he died a violent death</u>.

3. _____   Close analysis of this hand injury shows that <u>the wound was already beginning to heal at the time of his death</u>.

4. _____   So it is unlikely <u>he injured his hand in his final days</u>.

5. _____   This meant that <u>he ate a big meal immediately before his death</u> …

6. _____   Scientists guessed that <u>the Iceman might have been resting after a meal when enemies attacked him from behind</u>.

7. _____   Perhaps the most likely explanation is that <u>the Iceman was fleeing an earlier battle, but thought he was safe at the moment of his murder</u>.

Frequently Asked Questions

How are the Student Book units organized?

Each unit consists of four main sections:

Reading 1, Video, Reading 2, Writing

The unit opens with an introduction to the unit theme. The reading passages and videos that follow, together with their corresponding exercises, build towards a final writing task that incorporates the skills, topics, and language presented in the unit.

Will my students be able to handle the themes in the book?

The content and language is graded so that students can come into the series with little or no background information.

Each unit starts with a *Think and Discuss* page. The questions get students thinking about the unit's theme. The *Explore the Theme* spread then formally introduces students to the theme. It makes use of short passages, statistics, infographics, and other images to ease students in.

As students progress through a unit, exercises and activities add further to students' knowledge of the theme. By the time students get to the writing task, they will have enough language and information to express in writing their own ideas about the topic.

How are *Readings 1* and *2* related?

The two readings offer different perspectives on the unit theme. They usually consist of contrasting text types, for example, one might be an explanatory magazine-type article with infographics, and the other an adapted interview. The variety of text types is designed to mirror the range of reading texts that learners will encounter in print and online.

How does the series build vocabulary skills?

Each reading passage contains eight to ten high-frequency vocabulary items (highlighted in blue). These are introduced in the *Preparing to Read* section, which focuses on developing students' ability to use contextual clues to determine meaning. Target words are then reinforced and recycled throughout subsequent units. In addition, *Vocabulary Extension* activities at the end of the Student Book expand on some of these target words by introducing useful collocations, highlighting different word forms, and presenting common prefixes, suffixes, and word roots.

How are reading and writing integrated in the series?

All of the sections and exercises in each unit are thematically linked. *Readings 1* and *2* and their corresponding activities present and reinforce ideas, vocabulary, and grammar that students will use in their *Writing Task*. For example, students may learn to understand pronoun reference in *Reading 1*, and then be taught to use pronouns to avoid repetition as part of the *Writing Task*. Or students may read about explorers in both reading passages, and then be asked to write about a place they would like to explore.

What is the writing process approach taken in this series?

Students learn early on that writing is re-writing. This is the premise of *Pathways'* process approach to writing. As students work through the pre-writing, writing, and post-writing activities in each unit, they draft and re-draft their assignments. By repeating this process as they progress through the units, students internalize the steps and gradually become more independent writers.

How does *Pathways* develop writing skills?

At the end of every unit, students complete a *Writing Task*. In Level 3, students develop their ability to write a wide range of essays, including opinion, narrative, and problem-solution essays.

A section called *Exploring Written English* helps to prepare students for the *Writing Task*, and contains the following features:

- The *Language for Writing* box highlights lexical or grammar points that are useful for that unit's writing task. Examples include using past forms for narrative descriptions and using parallel structures to join ideas in a sentence.
- The *Writing Skill* box teaches useful paragraph and essay-level writing skills. Early units explain simple concepts like writing strong introductory and concluding paragraphs. Subsequent units include other basic essay writing skills such as how to plan an essay using a T-chart.

The *Exploring Written English* section gives students the tools they need for their writing task, which they will perform in five stages:

Brainstorming, Planning, Drafting, Revising, Editing

Students are guided through these steps, working through a series of activities to help shape, structure, and fine-tune their writing. The *Revising* and *Editing* stages each include a guided practice task, using model examples. Students learn how to apply the principles in these practice tasks to their own writing.

The *MyELT* online workbook provides additional guided writing tasks that build on the skills and language that learners have developed in the Student Book unit.

Instructors may wish to refer to the Writing Assessment Rubric in the Teacher's Guide when assessing students' written work, or provide students with a copy of the rubric for them to do a peer assessment of their final drafts.

Pathways Reading, Writing, and Critical Thinking 3: Writing Assessment Rubric

Name: _____   Unit: _____

Criterion	Score of 4	Score of 3	Score of 2	Score of 1
Pre-writing and organization	☐ **Well organized** • Clear thesis and topic sentences • Supporting ideas are in a logical sequence • Strong conclusion	☐ **Good organization** • Clear thesis and topic sentences • Supporting ideas are in a mostly logical sequence • Good conclusion	☐ **Some organization** • Thesis and topic sentences are slightly unclear • Sequencing of supporting ideas is unclear • Weak conclusion	☐ **Lacks organization** • Weak or missing thesis and / or topic sentences • Lack of sequencing of supporting ideas • No conclusion
Content	☐ **Excellent supporting ideas that are appropriate to the task** • Supporting ideas are well explained and have enough details • Supporting ideas are related to the task goal and the paragraph's main idea	☐ **Strong supporting ideas that are appropriate to the task** • Supporting ideas are somewhat explained with a bit of detail • Supporting ideas are mostly related to the task goal and the paragraph's main idea	☐ **Good supporting ideas, but some are slightly unrelated to the task** • Supporting ideas are incomplete with little detail • Some supporting ideas are unrelated to the task or the paragraph's main idea	☐ **Weak supporting ideas or ideas that are unrelated to the task** • Supporting ideas are weak with little or no detail • Supporting ideas are unrelated to the task or the paragraph's main idea
Vocabulary	☐ **Wide range of vocabulary** • Appropriate and related to task • Effective use of less common words • Errors are minor and not frequent	☐ **Good range of vocabulary** • Appropriate and related to task • Good attempt to use less common words • Occasional errors, but meaning is still clear	☐ **Average range of vocabulary** • Mostly appropriate and related to task • Some attempt to use less common words • A number of errors that affect understanding	☐ **Limited range of vocabulary** • Minimally appropriate and related to task • Inaccurate use of target vocabulary • Frequent errors that greatly affect understanding
Sentence Structure and Grammar	☐ **Excellent sentence structure and language use** • Varied sentence structure • Very few grammatical errors in subject-verb agreement, verb tense agreement, use of conjunctions, etc.	☐ **Good sentence structure and language use** • Good variety of sentence structure • A few grammatical errors in subject-verb agreement, verb tense agreement, use of conjunctions, etc. that do not affect understanding	☐ **Average sentence structure and language use** • Little variety in sentence structure • A number of grammatical errors in subject-verb agreement, verb tense agreement, use of conjunctions, etc. that slightly affect understanding	☐ **Weak sentence structure and language use** • Simple or repetitive sentence structure • Many grammatical errors in subject-verb agreement, verb tense agreement, use of conjunctions, etc. that greatly affect understanding

Spelling and Punctuation	☐ **Excellent command of spelling and punctuation**
	• Few or no spelling errors
	• Correct use of punctuation:
	  ○ Capitalization of names and places and at the beginning of sentences
	  ○ Use of comma between clauses and where appropriate
	  ○ Use of period or question mark at the end of sentences
	  ○ Use of apostrophes for indicating possession
		☐ **Good command of spelling and punctuation**
		• Some spelling errors, but mostly with uncommon words
		• Mostly correct use of punctuation:
		  ○ Capitalization of names and places and at the beginning of sentences
		  ○ Use of comma between clauses and where appropriate
		  ○ Use of period or question mark at the end of sentences
		  ○ Use of apostrophes for indicating possession
			☐ **Average command of spelling and punctuation**
			• A number of spelling errors, some with common words
			• Some incorrect use of punctuation:
			  ○ Capitalization of names and places and at the beginning of sentences
			  ○ Use of comma between clauses and where appropriate
			  ○ Use of period or question mark at the end of sentences
			  ○ Use of apostrophes for indicating possession
				☐ **Weak command of spelling and punctuation**
				• Many spelling errors
				• Largely incorrect use of punctuation:
				  ○ Capitalization of names and places and at the beginning of sentences
				  ○ Use of comma between clauses and where appropriate
				  ○ Use of period or question mark at the end of sentences
				  ○ Use of apostrophes for indicating possession

Score				

Total score: ☐ / 20

USING THE TEACHER'S GUIDE

Each unit of this Teacher's Guide contains:

- Overviews of reading passages and videos
- Background information and key lesson points
- Teaching notes for each exercise
- Answer keys
- Follow-up questions and activities

Other features include:

Recommended Time Frames

Look out for the small clock icon with recommended times for completing various tasks. While the recommended total time required for each unit is about five class hours, this will of course vary depending on your particular teaching situation. Likewise, the time allocated for specific sections should be used more as a guide than as a rule. Refer to the pacing guides on the following page for a more detailed breakdown.

Ideas for ... EXPANSION

These contain suggestions for extra classroom activities that can be used when students need additional support, or when there is an opportunity to explore a different aspect of the unit theme.

In addition, this Teacher's Guide also contains:

Video Transcripts

Use these for a more detailed study of the video content. The scripts, for example, can be provided to students after they view the video as additional reading practice.

Graphic Organizers

There is a photocopiable graphic organizer for one of the reading passages in the unit. The organizers include concept maps, process diagrams, and note-taking charts that can be handed out to students before or after they read the passage, to help them organize key points.

PACING GUIDES

One unit of *Pathways 3* typically requires 4.5–6 hours to complete. All ten units require approximately 45–60 hours.

By setting aside portions of each unit as homework, or by using extension activities and ancillaries, a *Pathways* unit can be adapted to suit various course durations. Here are some examples:

Total course length: 45 hours	Total course length: 60 hours	Total course length: 90 hours	Total course length: 120 hours
30-week course: 1 × 90 minute class per week	**30-week course:** 2 × 60 min classes per week **15-week course:** 4 × 60 min classes per week	**30-week course:** 2 × 90 min classes per week	**30-week course:** 4 × 60 min classes per week
1 unit = 3 classes (4.5 hours) 10 units = 30 classes	1 unit = 6 classes (6 hours) 10 units = 60 classes	1 unit = 4 classes (6 hours) 10 units = 40 classes (out of 60 classes total) Remaining time = 30 hours *(extension activities / group projects / presentations / exams / reviews / school vacations)*	1 unit = 8 classes (8 hours) 10 units = 80 classes (out of 120 classes total) Remaining time = 40 hours *(extension activities / group projects / presentations / exams / reviews / school vacations)*
Class 1: Think and Discuss Explore the Theme Preparing to Read Reading 1 Understanding the Reading **Class 2:** Developing Reading Skills Video Preparing to Read Reading 2 **Class 3:** Understanding the Reading Exploring Written English Writing Task Unit Review	**Class 1:** Think and Discuss Explore the Theme Preparing to Read **Class 2:** Reading 1 Understanding the Reading **Class 3:** Developing Reading Skills Video **Class 4:** Preparing to Read Reading 2 Understanding the Reading **Class 5:** Understanding the Reading (continued) Exploring Written English **Class 6:** Writing Task Unit Review	**Class 1:** Think and Discuss Explore the Theme Preparing to Read Reading 1 Understanding the Reading **Class 2:** Developing Reading Skills Video Preparing to Read Reading 2 **Class 3:** Understanding the Reading Exploring Written English **Class 4:** Writing Task Unit Review Extension activities	**Class 1:** Think and Discuss Explore the Theme Preparing to Read Reading 1 **Class 2:** Understanding the Reading Developing Reading Skills **Class 3:** Video **Class 4:** Preparing to Read Reading 2 **Class 5:** Understanding the Reading **Class 6:** Exploring Written English **Class 7:** Writing task Unit Review **Class 8:** Extension activities / group projects
This option assumes that: – the first draft, and the revising and editing of drafts, are set as homework.		This option assumes that: There is enough time to complete the entire Student Book and extension activities / Ideas for Expansion in class. – The Teacher's Guide provides numerous follow-up questions and extension activities in each unit. – Online Workbook activities and ExamView unit quizzes can be set as homework.	This option assumes that: There is enough time to complete the entire Student Book and extension activities / Ideas for Expansion in class. – The Teacher's Guide contains numerous follow-up questions and extension activities. – Online Workbook activities and ExamView unit quizzes can be done in class or set as homework.

SOCIAL RELATIONSHIPS

ACADEMIC TRACK
Behavioral Science

ACADEMIC SKILLS
READING	Identifying main and supporting ideas
WRITING	Writing body paragraphs
GRAMMAR	Making comparisons
CRITICAL THINKING	Analyzing evidence

UNIT OVERVIEW
The theme of this unit is social interactions in the animal and human world. From social relationships in the wild to those in human workplaces, students learn about and discuss our similarities with animals.

- **READING 1:** Human behavior in the workplace shares a number of similarities with animal behavior in the wild.

- **VIDEO:** A wildlife organization cares for orphaned baby elephants so that they can eventually live with other elephants in the wild.

- **READING 2:** Three studies of animal behavior in the wild reveal some interesting insights about gender roles in the animal world.

Students draw on what they have read and watched to write two paragraphs comparing animal and human behavior. The unit prepares them for the writing task by introducing vocabulary to talk about social interactions, along with reviewing the basic concept of main ideas and supporting ideas in paragraphs. It teaches language for making comparisons, and how to organize body paragraphs in an essay. It also takes students through the steps of brainstorming and planning, and shows them how to revise and edit their paragraphs.

 THINK AND DISCUSS (page 1)

The photo shows a polar bear mother with her cubs, illustrating a strong social relationship. The title and questions help prepare students for the subject matter covered in the unit.
- Have students study the picture, title, and caption. Elicit the meaning of *cubs*. (In this case, *cubs* refers to the baby polar bears.)

- Discuss the photo as a class. What words describe the relationship they see in the picture? (warm, loving, caring, etc.)
- Discuss the questions as a class. For question **1**, elicit examples of animals that live in groups. Use this as an opportunity to review words for social units of animals: *pack* (dogs/wolves), *pride* (lions), *herd* (cows and other large mammals), *flock* (birds, sheep), *school* (fish, dolphins, whales), *swarm* (bees and other flying insects), *colony* (ants, penguins). For question **2**, ask students to reflect on animal and human social behavior in regard to groups and families. Note that students will be asked to compare animal and human behavior in their writing task at the end of the unit.

ANSWER KEY

THINK AND DISCUSS

Answers will vary. Possible answers:
1. Other animals that live in social groups include mammals such as horses, lions, elephants, wolves, dolphins, and whales; fish; insects such as bees, ants, and wasps; birds such as penguins, geese, and sparrows.
2. Many animals stay with their families when they are young, as humans do. Many animals take care of and protect others in their social groups. Animals that live in groups fight sometimes, just like humans.

 EXPLORE THE THEME (pages 2–3)

The opening spread highlights some similar behavioral characteristics between humans and other primates.
- Allow time for students to study the spread and answer the questions individually.
- Check answers as a class. For question **2**, ask students whether they think humans or animals are better communicators.

ANSWER KEY

EXPLORE THE THEME

A **1.** monkeys and apes
   2. Both humans and other primates communicate and use tools. Both also live in social groups where they care for one another and take care of their young.

B   treat; interact; care for

Reading 1

PREPARING TO READ *(page 4)*

A Building Vocabulary

Building Vocabulary exercises introduce students to key vocabulary items from the reading passage. The paragraph is related to the reading passage. It describes aggressive behavior in the workplace, motivations behind it, and how it can negatively affect a working environment. Students should use context from the sentences as clues to identify the part of speech of each vocabulary item and match each one to its definition.

- Have students work individually to complete the exercise.
- Check answers as a class. Elicit example sentences for each vocabulary item.

B Using Vocabulary

Students should practice using the new vocabulary items while answering the questions.

- Have students work in pairs to answer the questions. If necessary, provide some prompts to help with their discussion. (1. *I'd rather be … because …*; 2. *If I had an aggressive coworker, I'd probably …*)
- Check answers as a class. Elicit example answers from students.

C Brainstorming

Students should think of at least two ideas for each question. Offer students one or two examples before they begin. (Examples: work on a project team; help each other find food)

- Allow students time to brainstorm ideas in small groups.
- Discuss as a class. Create a large class Venn diagram on the board with examples of human and animal cooperation in social settings.

D Predicting

Predicting what a passage is about before reading it helps the reader understand the passage better later on. In this reading passage, the title, captions, and headings provide clues about the passage content.

- Allow students time to skim the title, captions, and headings.
- Have students work in pairs to write three ideas.
- Discuss answers as a class. Revisit this question after students have completed the reading.

Ideas for … EXPANSION

A vocabulary notebook is a great way for students to build their vocabularies. Demonstrate on the board how to write new words in the notebook, and include details such as *part of speech, meaning, translation,* and an *example sentence.* (Example: *criticize [verb]: to speak badly of something or someone. "The author criticized the new movie in the article.")*

1.01 Have students read the passage individually, or play the audio and have students read along.

OVERVIEW OF THE READING

The passage describes how human behavior in the office echoes primate behavior in the wild, as observed by Richard Conniff, author of *The Ape in the Corner Office*. For example, both humans and other primates use social networking to move up the ladder to improve their status. Ambitious individuals in both worlds make an effort to create social connections with leaders of their communities. In addition, aggressive behavior may be rewarded in the short run, but it leads to isolation in the long run.

Online search terms: Richard Conniff, The Ape in the Corner Office

60 MINS UNDERSTANDING THE READING
(*pages 8–9*)

A Understanding Purpose

Students are asked to determine the reasons why Conniff wrote his book *The Ape in the Corner Office*.
- Have students work individually to complete the activity.
- Check answers as a class. Discuss where students found the reasons.

B Summarizing

Students are asked to complete a summary of the reading.
- Have students work individually to complete the activity. Point out that each answer is only one word.
- Have students form pairs to compare answers.
- Discuss answers as a class. Ask what clues the students used to get their answers.

C Categorizing

This exercise requires students to group examples of workplace behavior and wild primate behavior.
- If necessary, review how to complete a Venn diagram. Make sure students understand that the overlapping section is for the behaviors that both animals and humans exhibit.
- Have students work individually to complete the activity.
- Have them form pairs to compare answers.
- Discuss answers as a class. If there is time, compare this Venn diagram with the one on the board that the class completed for exercise **C** of the *Preparing to Read* section.

D Critical Thinking: Analyzing Evidence

The *Critical Thinking* box explains evidence that authors use to support their arguments, such as examples, quotations from experts, and statistics. Discuss how this kind of evidence strengthens an essay or article. Tell students that evidence makes the content more believable to the reader. For the exercise, students are asked to refer back to sections of the reading to find evidence.
- Allow students time to refer to the passage to find the evidence. Note that the subheadings in the chart (e.g., statistics) indicate the type of evidence students should look for.
- Check answers as a class.

E Critical Thinking: Evaluating Evidence

Students are next asked to evaluate the evidence that they compiled in exercise **D**.
- Have students work in groups.
- Ask each member to identify which piece of evidence they think is the weakest and why.
- Then have group members discuss what kind of evidence could be added to make the argument stronger.
- Discuss answers as a class. Elicit responses from each group.

F Inferring Meaning

Students are asked to guess the meaning of a word from its context in the reading. Discuss why doing this can be better than relying on a dictionary. (Possible answer: Stopping to look up words can affect reading fluency and interfere with comprehension.) Note that students use a three-step process in this exercise. First, they find and underline the words in the passage. Second, they use context to deduce the meaning of the words. Third, they complete the definitions of the words.
- Have students underline the four words in the reading.
- Ask them to read the sentences around the one containing the target word.
- Have students work out the part-of-speech of the target word.
- Ask them to then complete the definitions.
- Check answers as a class.

G Critical Thinking: Reflecting

When reading someone's argument, it is useful for students to draw connections to what they already know. It will help them better evaluate the points presented.
- Have students write down their own answers individually before discussing them in pairs.
- Discuss answers as a class. Ask for volunteers to share any experiences that support or contradict the content of the reading passage.

UNDERSTANDING THE READING

A 1, 4 (See Paragraphs B and C.)

B (See Paragraph C.)

1. cooperate
2. conflict
3. networking
4. hierarchies
5. aggressive

C office workers: a, i

wild apes: e, f, h, j

Both: b, c, d, g

D **Cooperation versus Conflict:** Chimps spend about 5 percent of the day being aggressive, but 15 to 20 percent of the day grooming each other. (See Paragraph C.)

The Value of Networking: Research by Frans de Waal, a primatologist, shows that chimps often use their networking skills to strengthen their social status or to get ahead. (See Paragraph D.)

The Importance of Hierarchies: Young people speak softly and avoid eye contact; young chimps make themselves look smaller. (See Paragraph F.)

The Limits of Aggression: Human employees lose motivation and quit if treated aggressively; aggressive apes chase other apes away. (See Paragraph G.)

E Answers will vary. Possible answer: Adding an example from a specific case study could help strengthen the quote in *The Value of Networking*.

F 1. useful (Paragraph H: …*is more <u>beneficial</u> for both humans and primates*.)

2. competing (Paragraph E: *They see a main <u>rival</u> sitting*…)

3. frightened (Paragraph G: *People sometimes shout or <u>intimidate</u> others*…)

4. connected to (Paragraph D: *They create tight social <u>bonds</u>*…)

G Answers will vary. Possible answers: I speak politely when talking to my boss at my part-time job. / I once had an aggressive coworker who got promoted! Nobody liked him, but he was rewarded by the company.

DEVELOPING READING SKILLS
(page 10)

Reading Skill: Identifying Main and Supporting Ideas

The *Reading Skill* box explains that the main idea of a paragraph, which is expressed in its topic sentence, is supported with information to answer questions such as how, what, why, and when. Supporting ideas include examples, statistics, quotations, etc. Supporting ideas provide a more detailed explanation of the main idea and also make it more convincing. For example, quotations can be used to give an expert's opinion.

A Identifying Main and Supporting Ideas

Students are asked to read a paragraph and then identify its main idea and supporting ideas.
- Allow time for students to read the paragraph.
- Have them work individually to complete the exercise.
- Check answers as a class.

B Identifying Main and Supporting Ideas

Students are asked to think more deeply about their answers to exercise **A**.
- Have students work in pairs or in small groups. Ask them to discuss what helped them recognize a main idea versus a supporting idea.
- Then have them discuss what questions about the main idea are answered in the supporting idea.
- Discuss as a class. Elicit answers for each supporting detail. Ask whether all the other groups agree.

C Applying

Students are asked to identify the main ideas and supporting details in a paragraph from the reading. Note that there are two possible main ideas.
- Allow time for students to reread Paragraph G.
- Have students compare what they underlined with a partner.
- Check answers as a class.

DEVELOPING READING SKILLS

A   **1.** S;   **2.** S;   **3.** S;   **4.** (extra);   **5.** M

B   how: 1; what: 3; why: 2

C   Answers will vary. Possible answers:

Main Idea 1: Although cooperation is more common in groups, both humans and other primates sometimes use conflict in order to gain status.

Supporting Ideas: People sometimes shout or intimidate others to make a point or win an argument.; Apes show aggression by pounding their chests, screeching, or hitting trees.

OR

Main Idea 2: However, Conniff notes that conflict does not gain long-term success for either species.

Supporting Ideas: When bosses criticize their employees, treat them unfairly, or make their working lives difficult, employees become stressed, lose motivation, and quit their jobs.; When apes are aggressive, they chase other apes away.

Video

VIEWING: ELEPHANT ORPHANS
(pages 11–12)

Overview of the Video

Elephants are social creatures that live in herds. Baby elephants spend years living with their mothers in the wild. So when an elephant is orphaned, it is a challenge to provide it with what it needs to grow into a healthy, social adult. The David Sheldrick Wildlife Trust is an organization that has been caring for orphaned baby elephants for over 40 years. Caretakers stay with the baby elephants all day and night to give them the same amount of social interaction that they would have in the wild. The organization aims to re-introduce the orphans back into the wild eventually. As a species, elephants are being threatened by human activities such as poaching and urban development, which means any effort to save these orphans is an effort to save the species.

Online search terms: The David Sheldrick Wildlife Trust

BEFORE VIEWING

A Predicting

The photo shows the caretakers from The David Sheldrick Wildlife Trust feeding the elephants under their care.

- Have students read the photo caption and think about the kind of care baby elephants need (food, social interaction, etc.)
- Discuss answers as a class.

B Learning About the Topic

The paragraph prepares students for the video by familiarizing them with one of the major threats to elephant populations: poachers. Inform students that there is more than one answer to each question.

- Have students read the paragraph and answer the questions individually.
- Have them form pairs to check their answers.
- Initiate a class discussion. Ask whether students have ever seen an item made from ivory. What is the attitude in their country toward the ivory trade?

C Vocabulary in Context

This exercise introduces students to some of the key words used in the video. Students use context to deduce the meaning of the words.

- Have students work on the exercise individually.
- Have them form pairs to check their answers.
- Discuss as a class. Elicit example sentences for each word.

BEFORE VIEWING

A Answers will vary. Possible answer: The elephants need someone to feed them and interact with them.

B Answers will vary. Possible answers:

1. In some cultures, products made from ivory are thought to have special significance. / Some people are unaware of the illegal hunting of elephants for the purpose of collecting ivory.

2. Stricter laws can be set to reduce poaching. / Governments and organizations could make people more aware of the illegal ivory trade and discourage them from buying ivory products.

C 1. maternal

2. slaughter (Note: The word *slaughter* usually refers to killing in an especially violent or cruel way.)

3. caretaker

4. reintroduction

WHILE VIEWING

A ▶ Understanding Main Ideas

Have students read the items before playing the video.
- Have them complete the task while the video is playing.
- Check answers as a class. Elicit some other challenges that the caretakers face.

B ▶ Understanding Details

Have students read the questions and write any answers they recall from the first viewing before playing the video a second time.
- Play the video again. Have them complete the task while the video is playing.
- Check answers as a class.

WHILE VIEWING

A c

B 1. milk / food / social interaction / play

2. The caretakers stay with the elephants 24 hours a day. / Blankets are used to mimic maternal warmth.

3. Both human babies and elephant babies like to play; they ignore your warnings about what not to do and where not to go; and both also need social interaction to feel safe.

AFTER VIEWING

A Reacting to the Video

Students are asked to think about how the shelter is able to help the elephants, as well as the shelter's limitations.
- Allow time for students to work individually to answer the questions.
- Have them discuss their answers in pairs.
- For question **1**, have a class discussion so students can express their ideas. For question **2**, have the class brainstorm ways in which The David Sheldrick Wildlife Trust helps or does not help stop poaching. Write ideas on the board.

B Critical Thinking: Synthesizing

Students draw on information from both the *Explore the Theme* section and the video to formulate their answers.
- Have students discuss their ideas in pairs.
- If time permits, discuss their ideas as a class.

AFTER VIEWING

A Answers will vary. Possible answers:

1. The elephants will face many dangers when they are reintroduced to the wild.

2. The Trust may help prevent poaching by educating others about the existence of baby elephants that have been orphaned because of poachers, but the video does not mention any specific efforts made to stop poachers directly.

B Answers will vary. Possible answers: Both primates and elephants share with humans a need for social interaction. / Both live in social groups or families.

Reading 2

PREPARING TO READ *(page 13)*

30 MINS

A Building Vocabulary

The sentences in the box contain ten vocabulary items that appear in the reading passage. Students should use contextual clues to deduce the meaning of the words.

- Have students complete the task individually.
- Check answers as a class. Elicit example sentences for each vocabulary item.

See Vocabulary Extension 1 in the Student Book for additional practice with pre-.

B Using Vocabulary

Students should use the new vocabulary items while discussing the questions.

- Have students work in pairs to answer the questions. If necessary, provide prompts to support their discussion. (1. *Establishing routines can help…*; 2. *When you live in an extended family, you…*)
- Check answers as a class. Elicit example answers from students.

C Predicting

Students are asked to read the title and headings to find a connection between the sections in the reading passage.

- Allow time for students to skim the title and headings.
- Have students form pairs to check their answers.

ANSWER KEY

PREPARING TO READ

A 1. generally

2. intense

3. extended family

4. social structure

5. gender (Note that *gender* mostly refers to social and cultural aspects of being male or female, not to biological sex.)

6. establish

7. discipline

8. observe

9. replace

10. previously

B Answers will vary. Possible answers:

1. Establishing a routine can help me with time management and help reduce stress in my life.

2. Some benefits of living in an extended family include having a lively household and having people to help take care of each other. Some drawbacks include lack of privacy and maybe more family arguments!

C a

 1.02 Have students read the passage individually, or play the audio and have students read along.

OVERVIEW OF THE READING

Three studies reveal interesting details about social relationships among different species, particularly in regard to gender. Although elephants are known for their strong matriarchal bonds, males also form their own social groups with hierarchies and strong social bonds. A study of gelada baboons reveals that it is the females who control the family group. Finally, a third study reveals that young chimpanzees express gender roles through their play activities. The studies were featured in articles published by *National Geographic*.

Online search terms: Chimp "Girls" Play With "Dolls" Too; King of the Hill? by Virginia Morrell

UNDERSTANDING THE READING
(pages 17–18)

60 MINS

A Understanding Main Ideas

Students are asked to identify the main idea of each section of the reading passage.

- Have students work individually to complete the activity.
- Check answers as a class. Ask students how they identified the main purpose of each section.

B Identifying Main and Supporting Ideas

Students are asked to identify the main and supporting ideas in Paragraphs D–F.

- Complete the first item as an example for the class.
- Then allow students time to work individually.
- Check answers as a class.

C Understanding Details

Students complete details about the passage, using no more than three words in each space.

- Allow students time to work individually.
- Check answers as a class. Discuss where students found the relevant information.

D Critical Thinking: Analyzing Evidence

Students practice the critical thinking skill introduced in the *Understanding the Reading* section in Reading 1.

- Have students work in pairs.
- Check answers as a class. For each piece of evidence, discuss briefly how it helps support the main ideas of each section. This prepares students for exercise **E**.

E Critical Thinking: Evaluating Evidence

Students evaluate the effectiveness of the evidence from the previous exercise.

- Have students work in pairs to share their opinions about the evidence from exercise **D**.
- If necessary, review what makes a piece of evidence convincing. (Convincing evidence is believable and clear, and supports the author's main idea.)

F Inferring Meaning

Students first find and underline the words in the passage. Then they use context to deduce the meaning of the words. Finally, they complete sentences using the words.

- Have students work in pairs to locate the words in the passage and deduce their meaning.
- Have them complete the sentences using the words.
- Check answers as a class.

G Critical Thinking: Synthesizing

Students draw on information from each section of the reading passage. They can also refer to Reading 1 for more information on chimps.

- Have students work individually to complete the chart.
- Then have students discuss their ideas in pairs.
- If time permits, discuss students' ideas as a class.

Ideas for ... EXPANSION

Have students work in small groups. Ask them to find out about another animal species with interesting gender roles. Allow groups time to go online and gather information. Have each group share with the class 2–3 interesting things about how gender roles influence the social structure of that species.

UNDERSTANDING THE READING

A 1. b;   **2.** a;   **3.** a

B   **Paragraph D:** M: (the) power, S2: during the day / every day, S3: their mate/mates

   Paragraph E: M: separate groups, S1: family male, S2: invite

   Paragraph F: M: replaced, S: stay on

C 1. status (See Paragraph C.)

   2. Older males / Older male elephants (See Paragraph C.)

   3. family male / primary male (See Paragraph D.)

   4. grandfather (See Paragraph F.)

   5. active play / climbing, jumping, etc. (See Paragraph H.)

   6. motherhood (See Paragraph I.)

D 1. study / research study

   2. primatologist

   3. caretaking

   4. 14; a hundred

E   Answers will vary. Possible answers:

   1. Yes, I think it is convincing because the study was done for 14 years and involved many different observations of the same behavior.

   2. I think the gelada study is the most convincing because there are many examples of the kind of behavior being explained.

F 1. pecking order (Paragraph C: *"in dry years, the strict pecking order they establish benefits…"*)

   2. mimicked/mimics/was mimicking (Paragraph H: *Kanyawara chimps played with sticks mimicked…*) (Note: The spelling of the verb *mimic* changes depending on form: *mimic, mimics, mimicked, mimicking*)

   3. offspring (Paragraph D: *…eight adult females, their offspring, and…*)

   4. in captivity (Paragraph G: *…rhesus monkeys often play with dolls in captivity.*)

G   **chimpanzees:** hierarchy is important, forming social bonds is important

   elephants: females control the group, hierarchy is important, forming strong bonds is important

   geladas: females control the group, forming social bonds is important (See *Explore the Theme* for importance of primate social bonds.)

Writing

OVERVIEW

In this section, students learn about the function of body paragraphs in an essay. The lesson starts by teaching language for making comparisons and then reviews the basic structure of an essay, focusing on body paragraphs. In the *Writing Task*, students apply what they have learned by writing two body paragraphs comparing the behavior of humans and another animal species. Students begin with a brainstorming exercise before they learn how to select, organize, and combine information. Finally, they check for common mistakes with comparison expressions.

 EXPLORING WRITTEN ENGLISH
(pages 19–21)

A Noticing

While completing the exercise, students should notice expressions used to show similarities and differences. This exercise is to be done before going over the information in the *Language for Writing* box.

• Have students complete the task individually. Tell them to pay close attention to the language used to help them differentiate the sentences.
• Check answers as a class.

Language for Writing: Making Comparisons

The *Language for Writing* box reviews expressions for making comparisons. Go over each expression and its use. Note that some expressions can be used at the beginning of a sentence or within a sentence. Highlight how commas should be used when some of these expressions appear at the start of a sentence, or within a sentence.

B Language for Writing

Students are asked to refer back to exercise **A** and underline the phrases used to indicate either similarity or difference.

• Have students complete the activity individually.
• Check answers as a class.

C Language for Writing

Students are asked to complete the sentences using words or phrases for expressing similarities or differences. Tell students to refer to the *Language for Writing* box, if necessary.

• Have students work individually to answer the questions.
• Check answers as a class.

D Language for Writing

Students use the expressions for making comparisons and the chart from Reading 2 to write three comparison sentences.

• Explain that students can choose any pair of animals to write about, and that it is all right to vary the pairs (or not) in each sentence.
• Have students work individually to write the sentences.
• Have them form pairs to compare answers. Alternatively, check answers as a class, eliciting sample sentences from students.

ANSWER KEY

EXPLORING WRITTEN ENGLISH

A 1. S
   2. S
   3. D
   4. S
   5. D

LANGUAGE FOR WRITING

B 1. both
   2. Similarly
   3. In contrast
   4. Likewise
   5. Unlike

C 1. In contrast,
   2. Likewise, / Similarly,
   3. , while / , whereas
   4. , on the other hand,
   5. Similarly, / Likewise,

D Answers will vary. Possible answers:

Forming social bonds is important for both elephants and primates.

Elephants live in a matriarchal family. Similarly, gelada families are led by females.

Unlike female elephants, female chimpanzees don't necessarily have the most power in their family group.

Writing Skill: Writing Body Paragraphs

The *Writing Skill* box introduces the typical structure of an essay, with a focus on body paragraphs in comparison essays. Each body paragraph expresses one main idea to support the thesis of an essay. In a comparison essay, the body paragraphs may focus only on similarities or only on differences, or they can be split to have one focus on similarities and one on differences. Note that an example body paragraph comparing wolves and dogs is in exercise **E**.

E Analyzing Body Paragraphs

Students read an example body paragraph in an essay comparing dogs and wolves. Tell students to use the tips in the *Writing Skill* box to answer the questions about the body paragraph.

- Allow students time to read the paragraph.
- Have students work on the exercises individually.
- Have them form pairs to check their answers.
- Discuss the answers as a class. Go over each answer in item 3 to review the different parts of the paragraph.

ANSWER KEY

WRITING SKILL

E 1. a difference

2. their relationships with humans

3. a. One way that dogs and wolves differ is in their relationships with humans.

b. Dogs are generally friendly and helpful around humans.

c. Wolves, on the other hand, are shy and fearful of humans.

d. For example, dogs helped early humans hunt.

e. One reason for this is that wolves are generally afraid of anything that is unfamiliar.

WRITING TASK (page 22)

A Brainstorming

Remind students that brainstorming is a useful first step for gathering ideas before writing. Read the *Goal* box aloud so students are familiar with the writing task before brainstorming. Students are asked to compare the behavior of one animal species with human behavior. When brainstorming, students should list as many ideas that closely relate to the animal's behavior as possible. Ideas should be briefly worded. They need not be listed in any order.

- Explain that students can use any of the animal species that they read about in the unit or another species that they are familiar with.
- Tell students to use the questions in the exercise to help them brainstorm.
- Allow students time to work individually and write their ideas.
- Have them share their ideas in pairs and give each other feedback.

B Planning

Students should choose two points of comparison to write about. As students have not been introduced to the thesis statement yet, two partially completed ones have been provided. They are to complete the suitable thesis statement. Remind students that complete sentences are not necessary for their outline details. It is more important to focus on organizing their information.

- Allow time for students to complete their outlines individually. Provide assistance as needed.

C First Draft

Have students write a first draft of their paragraphs based on their outline.

- Allow time for students to complete the task individually. Provide assistance as needed. Refrain from error correction at this point.

WRITING TASK

A Answers will vary. Possible answers:

Animal: elephant

Notes: strict social hierarchy, cooperation over conflict, matriarchal, travel together, young ones stay with mothers for a long time

B Answers will vary. Possible answers:

Thesis Statement: Elephants and humans are similar in some ways, but different in others. They both form important social bonds with others, but they differ in terms of social structures.

Body Paragraph 1

Topic Sentence: In both elephant herds and human families, social bonds are key.

Supporting Ideas/Details: Elephants stay with their mothers for many years, as humans do; older male elephants teach younger males, etc.

Body Paragraph 2

Topic Sentence: Unlike humans, elephants tend to interact mostly with those of the same gender.

Supporting Ideas/Details: Adult female elephants cooperate to raise families together; adult male elephants live in groups with other males.

REVISING PRACTICE *(page 23)*

The *Revising Practice* box contains an exercise that demonstrates several ways students can improve their first drafts.

- Allow students time to analyze the two drafts and complete the exercise.
- Check answers as a class. Ask students to identify each change and explain how it makes the revised draft stronger.

D Revised Draft

Students should apply the revision techniques used in the *Revising Practice* box to their own drafts, where applicable.

- Explain to students that they will be using the questions as a guide for checking and improving their drafts.
- As a class, go over the questions carefully to make sure students understand them.
- Allow students time to revise their paragraphs.

EDITING PRACTICE

The *Editing Practice* box trains students to spot and correct common errors related to comparison expressions. As a class, go over the information in the box carefully to make sure students understand what to look out for.

- Allow students time to complete the exercise individually.
- Check answers as a class by asking students to read their corrected sentences aloud and explain the errors.

ANSWER KEY

REVISING PRACTICE

c, d, a, b

EDITING PRACTICE

1. The use of tools among gorillas <u>is</u> similar to the use of tools among chimpanzees.
2. Dogs are not capable of using language. In <u>contrast</u>, some apes are able to communicate using human sign language.
3. Horses help farmers by pulling carts. <u>Likewise</u>, dogs help by herding sheep.
4. Cats in the wild have to hunt for food. House <u>cats</u>, on the other hand, get their food from humans.
5. Chimpanzee mothers and daughters form strong bonds. <u>Similarly</u>, adult female elephants form close relationships with young females in the family.

E Final Draft

Have students apply the skills taught in *Editing Practice* to their own revised drafts and check for any other errors.

- Allow students time to edit their drafts.
- Walk around and monitor students as they work. Provide assistance as needed.
- Collect their work once they have completed it.
- For the next class, show anonymous examples of good paragraphs and common errors.

Ideas for ... EXPANSION

Have students work in groups of three to review and edit each other's paragraphs further. Ask each group member to read another's paragraphs and try to do the following:

- Correct one error in grammar, spelling, etc.
- Give one compliment.
- Give one piece of feedback to help improve the paragraphs.

Allow students time to read each other's paragraphs, take notes, and then discuss their feedback.

UNIT REVIEW

Students can work in groups on this recap of the unit. For question **1**, encourage students to use the target vocabulary words when appropriate. For questions **2** and **3**, encourage them to check the relevant pages of the unit for answers.

- Allow students time to answer the three questions in groups.
- Ask each group to present its answer for question **1**.

SCIENCE AND INVESTIGATION

ACADEMIC TRACK

Technology / Genetics

ACADEMIC SKILLS

READING	Identifying a sequence of events
WRITING	Writing a summary
GRAMMAR	Paraphrasing
CRITICAL THINKING	Analyzing levels of certainty

UNIT OVERVIEW

The theme of this unit is how technology helps scientists solve mysteries, particularly in regard to crime. From modern unsolved cases to ancient mysteries, students learn how technology helps us uncover many hidden truths.

- **READING 1:** Three formerly unsolved cases get solved with the help of modern technology.
- **VIDEO:** An ancient murder in the mountains is explained more fully, and scientists learn useful information that can help us today.
- **READING 2:** After discovering the Egyptian pharaoh King Tutankhamun's tomb, archaeologists were able to use technology to learn more about his death, his life, and his family.

Students draw on what they have read and watched to write two paragraphs that summarize sections of a reading passage in the unit. The unit prepares them for the writing task by introducing vocabulary for talking about crimes and technology, as well as teaching language for describing time. It also teaches students ways of paraphrasing information and how to write a summary. Finally, it takes students through the steps of brainstorming and planning, and shows them how to revise and edit their summaries.

THINK AND DISCUSS *(page 25)*

The scene shows a picture of the results of a CT scan of the mummy of King Tutankhamun. Students will read more about this investigation in Reading 2. The title and questions help prepare students for the unit's theme.

- Have students study the picture, title, and captions. Elicit the meaning of *investigation* (an organized examination) and *crime* (an illegal activity).
- Discuss the photo as a class. Whose skull is pictured in the scan? (King Tut: His name is in the top left corner of the screen and in the caption.)

- Discuss the two questions as a class. For question **1**, elicit examples of some kinds of technology that assist in the investigation of crimes (for example, fingerprinting, CT scans, DNA matching, CCTV footage, etc.). For question **2**, ask students to briefly share any examples they know of crimes that were solved thanks to technology. These could be famous cases or local cases that they know about.

ANSWER KEY

THINK AND DISCUSS

Answers will vary. Possible answers:

1. Technology can reveal more evidence that helps match a criminal to a crime. Technology can be used to interpret evidence that is too small for the human eye to see.
2. In 2018, police solved a murder case after they found a photo of the suspect and the victim on social media. The murder weapon had matched an item on the suspect in the photo.

EXPLORE THE THEME *(pages 26–27)*

The opening spread explains DNA and DNA phenotyping in more detail. This new technology helps investigators identify some basic characteristics of a criminal's appearance.

- Allow time for students to study the spread and answer the questions individually.
- Check answers as a class.

ANSWER KEY

EXPLORE THE THEME

A 1. eye color, natural hair color, shape of facial features, geographic ancestry

   2. age, weight, dyed hair color, facial hair

B   suspect; commit; determine (Note: The verb *commit* is used in the unit primarily in reference to criminal behavior—*commit a crime; commit murder, commit theft,* etc.).

Reading 1

PREPARING TO READ *(page 28)*

A Building Vocabulary

The paragraphs describe two common forms of technology used in solving crimes: CT scanning and fingerprinting. Students should use context from the sentences as clues to match the vocabulary items to their definitions. A couple of words have similar definitions, so students should try to differentiate them using the part of speech.

- Have students work individually to complete the exercise.
- Check answers as a class. Elicit example sentences for each vocabulary item.

B Using Vocabulary

Students should use the new vocabulary items while discussing the questions.

- Have students work in pairs to answer the questions. If necessary, provide some prompts to assist with their discussion. (1. *Some skills police detectives need are … This is because they need to …*; 2. *I think I'd be great / I don't think I'd be great at investigating a crime or mystery because …*)
- Check answers as a class. Elicit example answers from students.

C Predicting

In this reading passage, the first paragraph and subheadings give useful clues about the passage's content. Students are also encouraged to think about how technology could be used in solving the cases in the passage.

- Allow students time to skim the first paragraph and subheadings.
- Ask students to think about the questions before discussing them in pairs.
- Discuss answers as a class. Revisit this exercise after students have completed the reading.

ANSWER KEY

PREPARING TO READ

A 1. heals   5. examine
    2. reveal   6. analysis
    3. mysteries   7. prove
    4. detectives

B Answers will vary. Possible answers:

1. Police detectives need to be good at paying attention to small details. They also need to be good at seeing possible connections between clues to solve a crime.

2. I don't think I'd be great at investigating a mystery because I often forget details. / I think I'd be good at investigating mysteries because I like solving puzzles.

C Answers will vary. Correct answers: The crimes discussed are robbery and murder. DNA matching from humans and plants, as well as CT imaging technology, helped detectives uncover details that led to the cases being solved.

 1.03 Have students read the passage individually, or play the audio and have students read along.

OVERVIEW OF THE READING

The passage describes three criminal cases where technology played a part in uncovering clues, from a recent robbery case to a murder that occurred over 5,000 years ago. In the first case, a leech that attached itself to a robber provides detectives with DNA evidence that they are able to finally match years later. In the second, plant DNA on a man's car leads to his conviction for a murder. In the third, CT imaging on an ancient mummy shows scientists that the man was killed by an arrow to his back. The passage content is based on articles that appeared on *National Geographic*'s news website.

Online search terms: Crime-Fighting Leech Fingers Perp, Iceman Autopsy, Iceman murder

UNDERSTANDING THE READING *(pages 32–33)*

A Understanding Main Ideas

Students are asked to indicate how technology helped researchers solve each crime.

- Have students work individually to complete the activity.
- Check answers as a class. Discuss where students found the answers.

B Understanding Details

Students are asked to identify each piece of information as true, false, or not given. The exercise is based on information in Paragraphs D and E.

- Have students work individually to complete the activity.
- Check answers as a class.
- Elicit where in the reading passage students found the relevant information.

C Categorizing

This exercise requires students to identify the pieces of evidence that are related to each crime.

- If necessary, review how to fill in a mind map. Make sure students understand how each bubble connects to the next. Explain that their answers (a–g) only go in the "Evidence" bubbles.
- Have students work individually to complete the activity.
- Have them form pairs to compare answers.
- Discuss answers as a class. Which evidence was most crucial for solving each crime?

D Critical Thinking: Analyzing Certainty

The *Critical Thinking* box explains language used to express levels of certainty. If necessary, draw a chart on the board with example words in these categories: *Factual/Certain*, *Mostly Certain*, and *Not Certain*. It will help students as they complete exercises **D** and **F**. In this exercise, students identify the writer's level of certainty in sentences from the reading passage.

- Allow students time to complete the exercise individually. Note that students do not need to refer to the reading passage to complete the exercise.
- Check answers as a class. Elicit the words or phrases that helped students determine the writer's level of certainty in each sentence.

E Critical Thinking: Analyzing Certainty

Students reread two parts of the passage to find examples of different levels of certainty used by the writer.

- Allow students enough time to go back and carefully check the passage.
- Tell students to underline the sentence and circle the word that indicates the level of certainty.
- Have students compare and discuss their answers in pairs.
- Discuss answers as a class. Ask for volunteers to share their examples from the passage.

F Critical Thinking: Evaluating

Students are next asked to evaluate the evidence from the reading passage and draw their own conclusions about the Iceman. What really happened to him?

- Have students work alone to write notes before they discuss their ideas in pairs or small groups.
- Have group members or partners discuss the evidence and their ideas and conclusions.
- Discuss answers as a class. Have each group present their ideas to the class about what happened to the Iceman.

ANSWER KEY

UNDERSTANDING THE READING

A 1. d (See Paragraph C.)

2. a (See Paragraph E.)

3. e (See Paragraph G.)

B 1. T (Explanation: Paragraph D: *...police found a pager at the scene of the crime that led them to a suspect.*)

2. NG (Explanation: There is no information about them being friends or strangers.)

3. NG (Explanation: There is no information about when he bought the truck.)

4. F (Explanation: Paragraph D: *The suspect admitted to giving the suspect a ride...*)

5. T (Explanation: Paragraph E: *This proved that the truck had definitely been to the crime scene...*)

C Australia robbery evidence: c, e, i, j

Arizona murder evidence: a, f, g, h, l

Iceman murder evidence: b, d, k

D 1. 2 (*believe*)   **5.** 3 (*meant*)

2. 3 (*clearly show*)   **6.** 1 (*might*)

3. 3 (*shows*)   **7.** 1 or 2 (*perhaps / most likely*)

4. 2 (*unlikely*)

E Answers will vary. Possible answers:

Certain: (Paragraph C) *This <u>proved</u> that the suspect was at the scene of the crime*; (Paragraph E) *...the geneticist <u>determined</u> that its DNA matched the one on the truck.*

Less certain: (Paragraph B) *The detectives thought the leech <u>could have</u> attached itself to one of the robbers...;* (Paragraph D) *And indeed, a palo verde tree at the scene of the crime looked like a truck <u>might have</u> hit it.*

F Answers will vary. Possible answers:

I think he was by himself. Some thieves were planning to steal his valuables, and they shot an arrow into his back. Since he was alone and not many people go to that area, he gradually became buried in the snow.

Reading Skill: Identifying a Sequence of Events

The *Reading Skill* box presents words and expressions that indicate how events relate to one another in a time sequence. Time markers can show whether an event happened before, after, or at the same time as another event. Recognizing these expressions will help students understand a sequence of events more quickly when they are scanning for information.

A Analyzing

Students are asked to look back at the reading passage and find the words that indicate a sequence of events. This exercise refers to Paragraphs B and C.

- Allow students time to look at the reading. Ask them to circle the words that indicate a sequence of time. Identify one time marker as an example, if necessary.
- Have students form pairs to compare their answers.

B Identifying a Sequence

Students are asked to put the events in Paragraphs B and C in the correct order.

- Have students work in pairs. Tell them to go through each event together and identify its place on the timeline.
- Point out that one event (a) is already given on the timeline.
- Check answers as a class. Elicit the words from the reading that helped students understand the sequence of events on the timeline.

ANSWER KEY

DEVELOPING READING SKILLS

A Paragraph B: in 2009; eight-year-old robbery case; in 2001; soon after; while; then

Paragraph C: Eight years later; after; 2001

B d, e, f, g, a, c, h, b

Video

Overview of the Video

A mummy found in 1991 in the Ötztal Alps turns out to be a 5,000-year-old unsolved crime. With the help of technology, scientists now believe the man was shot from behind with an arrow. They are hoping to find even more evidence to piece together this crime puzzle in the future. In addition to helping to explain the man's death, technology has helped scientist Albert Zink find out more about the Iceman's life. The video features Albert Zink as he talks about the research on the Iceman and the valuable information we can learn from him.

Online search terms: Albert Zink, National Geographic, Iceman heart disease, Onward: A 5,300-Year-Old Mummy with Keys to the Future

BEFORE VIEWING

A Learning About the Topic

The paragraph prepares students for the video by providing them with a list of information about the Iceman. It then asks them to think about what else they may want to know about the ancient mystery.

- Have students read the information individually.
- Have them work in pairs to answer the questions and share their ideas.
- Initiate a class discussion. Ask for volunteers to share their answers to question **2**.

B Vocabulary in Context

This exercise introduces students to some of the key words used in the video. Students use context to deduce the meaning of the words.

- Have students work on the exercise individually.
- Have them form pairs to check their answers.
- Discuss answers as a class. Elicit example sentences for each word.

BEFORE VIEWING

A   Answers will vary. Possible answers:

1. Easily visible items probably included his clothes, tattoos, tools, or anything that he had on him that was mummified with him. With technology, more detailed information about his age, facial features, height, and living relatives was obtained.

2. Answers will vary. Possible answers: Why was he in the mountains? Did his enemies kill him? Did he have a family?

B 1. nutrition

2. preserve

3. insight

4. gene

WHILE VIEWING

A ▶ **Understanding Main Ideas**

Have students read the items silently before you play the video.

- Have them complete the task while the video is playing.
- Check answers as a class.

B ▶ **Understanding Details**

Have students read the question and write any answers they recall from the first viewing before playing the video a second time.

- Play the video again. Have students complete the task while the video is playing.
- Check answers as a class.

WHILE VIEWING

A   2, 3, 4, 5 (Explanation: *Such an old mummy. It is the only one in this region that we have here in this region of such a high age; I think the Iceman is so special because on the one hand, he's perfectly preserved and he really gives us unique insights into this time that we don't know so much about; He contains a lot of information, also on different diseases; the Iceman is one of our ancestors, and it is very interesting to understand also the past and where we came from and how they already were able to adapt to the environment.*)

B   Answers may vary. Possible answers:

how he died / why he died / whether there are other mummies nearby / who killed him

AFTER VIEWING

A **Reacting to the Video**

Students are asked to think about the ethical issue of doing research on a human body—one that is mummified and over 5,000 years old.

- Allow time for students to think about their answers and make notes if necessary.
- Have them discuss their answers in pairs. Encourage students to use the prompts provided to share their views.
- Discuss their answers as a class. Make sure students understand that there is no right or wrong answer here, and every opinion is valued.

B **Critical Thinking: Synthesizing**

Students compare information from Reading 1 and the video to decide how certain they feel about the circumstances of the Iceman's death.

- Read the question aloud. Explain that students should use words and phrases that express levels of certainty in their discussions.
- Have students work in small groups to share their ideas and opinions. Ask them to support their opinions with reasons.
- If time permits, discuss their ideas as a class.

AFTER VIEWING

A   Answers will vary. Possible answers:

Yes, I think it is necessary for scientific research. The Iceman's body could give us valuable information that helps us better understand ourselves and the world. / I don't agree with doing research on a human body. I think they should respect his body instead.

B   Answers will vary. Possible answers:

I think it's likely that that he died from being shot by an arrow, but the reason for his murder is still unclear. Were his attackers stealing from him? Did they get in a fight earlier in the day?

Reading 2

PREPARING TO READ *(page 37)*

A Building Vocabulary

In this exercise, sentences that explain the meaning of key words from the reading passage are provided. Students should use these to help them complete the exercise.
- Have students complete the task individually. Tell students to change the form of the words as needed to complete the sentences.
- Check answers as a class. Elicit example sentences for each vocabulary item.

See Vocabulary Extension 2 in the Student Book for additional practice with -ist.

B Using Vocabulary

Students should use the new vocabulary items while discussing the two questions.
- Have students work in pairs to answer the questions. If necessary, provide prompts to initiate their discussions. (1. *I think archaeologists may want to know …*; 2. *It is probably challenging to obtain evidence because …*)
- Check answers as a class. Elicit example answers from students.

C Predicting

Students are asked to read the title and headings to identify two mysteries the passage focuses on.
- Allow time for students to skim the title and headings.
- Have students check their answers in pairs. Revisit the exercise after students have completed the reading.

ANSWER KEY

PREPARING TO READ

A 1. unclear

  2. mentions/mentioned, archaeologist

  3. combination

  4. suffered from, Moreover

  5. carried out, obtain

  6. sample, identity

B Answers will vary. Possible answers:

  Archaeologists are trying to learn about human life in the past to help scientists understand more about human life today.

  Archaeologists deal with very old objects, including human remains, so it's difficult to obtain proper evidence. First, it's hard to find these objects. Second, the condition of the discoveries is often not great.

C 2, 3

 1.04 Have students read the passage individually, or play the audio and have students read along.

OVERVIEW OF THE READING

The passage is based on an article by Egyptian archaeologist Zahi Hawass. In it, he explains his team's efforts to uncover the mystery behind the death of the young Egyptian monarch King Tutankhamun (often referred to as King Tut), one of the most famous pharaohs in history. He describes the steps followed and the technology used to investigate King Tut's cause of death, and he provides additional details about Tut's family, which were revealed during the investigation. The passage is an excerpt from the article *King Tut's Family Secrets*, published in *National Geographic* magazine.

Online search terms: Zahi Hawass, King Tut's Family Secrets

UNDERSTANDING THE READING *(pages 41–42)*

A Understanding Main Ideas

Students identify the paragraph that corresponds to each main idea.
- Have students work individually to complete the activity. Allow them time to look back at the passage.
- Check answers as a class. Ask students where they found the main idea in each paragraph.

B Understanding Details

Students are asked to identify each piece of information as true, false, or not given.
- Have students work individually to complete the exercise.
- Have them form pairs to check their answers.
- Check answers as a class. Discuss where students found the relevant information.

C Sequencing

Students practice the reading skill introduced earlier in the unit. They are asked to put the sequence of events from the reading passage in the correct order.
- Allow students time to refer back to the reading. Remind students to look for time markers to help them identify the correct order of events.
- Check answers as a class. Discuss where students found the relevant information.

D Inferring Meaning

Students first find and underline the target words in the passage. Then they use context to figure out what the words mean. Lastly, they write their own definition for each word.

• Have students work in pairs to locate the words in the passage and deduce their meaning.
• Have them discuss what they think each word means before they write their definitions.
• Check answers as a class. Note that definitions will differ slightly based on word choice but are acceptable if the meanings are correct.

E Critical Thinking: Analyzing Certainty

Students practice the critical thinking skill introduced in the *Understanding the Reading* section in Reading 1.

• Have students work in pairs to look back at Reading 2 and find a sentence that is certain and one that is less certain. Review the words and phrases indicating levels of certainty, if necessary.
• Discuss answers as a class. Ask each pair to read the information that they chose from the reading, identify its level of certainty, and explain the reason.

F Critical Thinking: Analyzing Certainty

Students are asked to draw conclusions about the research based on what Hawass has written about the reasons for Tut's death.

• Have students work individually to answer question **1**. Ask them to look back at the reading and find each health issue mentioned by Hawass that may have been a cause of death. Tell them to pay careful attention to word choice in regard to level of certainty as they read.
• Have them compare their answers to question **1** in pairs, then ask them to discuss their answers to question **2**.
• Check answers as a class. Do they think Hawass has solved this mystery? How certain do they think Hawass is about his own conclusions?

G Critical Thinking: Synthesizing

Students draw on information from the two reading passages and the video to formulate their answers.

• Have students work in pairs or small groups to complete the Venn diagram.
• Check answers as a class.

ANSWER KEY

UNDERSTANDING THE READING

A
1. E   4. H
2. K   5. D
3. C   6. F

B
1. T (Explanation: Paragraph J: *While the data are still incomplete, our study also suggests that one of the mummified fetuses is Tutankhamun's daughter and that the other may also be his child.*)
2. F (Explanation: The family tree infographic shows that Tuyu was his great-grandmother.)
3. NG (Explanation: His height is not mentioned in the passage.)
4. T (Explanation: Paragraph K: *Tutankhamun's clubbed foot and bone disease may therefore have been because he had a genetic predisposition.*)
5. F (Explanation: Paragraph L: *After Tutankhamun's death, a new dynasty came to power.*)

C   a, b, c, e, g, d, f

D
1. honor (verb): to respect
2. partial (adjective): incomplete, not whole
3. infant (noun): a newborn baby
4. siblings (plural noun): brothers or sisters

E   Answers will vary. Possible answers:

More certain: (Paragraph G) *…10 other mummies we believed were members of his family.* / (Paragraph J) *…our study also suggests that one of the mummified fetuses is Tutankhamun's daughter…*

Less certain: (Paragraph J) *One of these may be the mother of the infant mummies… / …she was the daughter of Akhenaten and his wife, Nefertiti, and therefore probably was Tutankhamun's half-sister.*

F
1. 2, 3, 4, 5, 6 (See Paragraph K.)
2. Answers will vary. Possible answer: Maybe not. Hawass uses the modal *may* when discussing the possible causes of King Tut's death in Paragraph K, so I don't think Hawass' team has completely solved the mystery.

G   Answers will vary. Possible answers:

Both: Scientists used technology such as DNA analysis and CT imaging to examine the bodies. / Scientists tried to determine Tutankhamun's and the Iceman's family backgrounds. / Both Tutankhamun and the Iceman had genetic predispositions.

Examination of Tutankhamun: More information in the form of other mummies was available for scientists to study Tutankhamun.

Examination of the Iceman: Scientists hope to use information from the Iceman to better deal with diseases.

Writing

OVERVIEW

In this section, students learn how to write a summary. The lesson starts by teaching a few methods for paraphrasing, and then goes on to introduce the main steps in summarizing. In the *Writing Task*, students apply these lessons by writing and revising summaries of two sections of Reading 1. Students begin with a brainstorming exercise, before selecting the most important ideas and organizing them in an outline. Students then write drafts of their summaries, improve their drafts, and correct common mistakes related to using synonyms.

 EXPLORING WRITTEN ENGLISH
(pages 43–45)

A Noticing

While completing the exercise, students should notice some of the techniques for paraphrasing (combining ideas, changing the word to a synonym, changing the part of speech). This exercise is to be done before going over the information in the *Language for Writing* box.

• Have students complete the task individually.
• Check answers as a class. For each question, go over the original and paraphrased versions to look at the differences.

Language for Writing: Paraphrasing

The *Language for Writing* box introduces three paraphrasing techniques that can be used when writing a summary: combine ideas, use synonyms, and change parts of speech. Go over each technique and how to use it. Explain that paraphrasing techniques help us avoid copying the author's original language. If necessary, explain why plagiarism must be avoided.

B Language for Writing

Students practice one of the techniques of paraphrasing by selecting the best choice for a synonym.

• Quickly review with students that a synonym has a very similar meaning to the original word. Remind students that it is important to consider the sentence context when they are choosing synonyms.
• Have students complete the activity individually. Allow the use of a dictionary or thesaurus, if needed.
• Check answers as a class.

C Language for Writing

Students practice two of the techniques for paraphrasing by changing the part of speech of a word and choosing an appropriate synonym.

• Have students complete the activity individually.
• Check answers as a class, looking closely together at how each sentence has been paraphrased.

Writing Skill: Writing a Summary

The *Writing Skill* box introduces the main steps in writing a summary. Before going over the information in the box, explain that summaries are useful for both readers and writers. As we do research or study, rephrasing what we have read in our own words helps us remember it better and also helps us avoid copying the author's language. Then go over the steps of writing a summary as outlined in the box.

D Writing Skill

Students are asked to refer to the "Researchers Discover Gender-Driven Play in Chimps" section of Reading 2 in Unit 1 for this exercise. Tell students to review the content and then put the events in the summary in the correct order.

• Allow students time to reread the section.
• Have students work on the exercise individually.
• Have them form pairs to check their answers.
• Discuss as a class. Point out that these particular points were chosen as they are important ideas in the section, and summaries should only contain the main points.

WRITING SKILL

D **a.** 1
 b. 7
 c. 5
 d. 3
 e. 4
 f. 6
 g. 2

 WRITING TASK *(page 46)*

A Brainstorming

Read the *Goal* box aloud so students are familiar with the writing task before brainstorming. The aim is to summarize two different sections from a reading passage in the unit, one paragraph for each section.

- Explain that students should do their brainstorming from memory. Tell them NOT to look at the sections yet. Remind them that short notes are acceptable.
- As they make notes, encourage them to use their own words.
- Allow them time to read the sections and compare their notes with the original information.

B Planning

Students complete the outline. For each summarized section, they should write a topic sentence and note the important ideas.

- Remind students to use synonyms, change parts of speech, and combine sentences when necessary.
- Allow time for students to complete their outlines individually. Provide assistance as needed.

C First Draft

Have students write first drafts of their summaries based on their outlines.

- Allow time for students to complete the task individually. Provide assistance as needed. Refrain from error correction at this point.

WRITING TASK

A   Answers will vary. Possible answers:

Notes from *A Body in the Mountains*:

Iceman was killed over 5,000 years ago; body was preserved by ice; CT scanning showed that he was shot by an arrow from behind; careful examination showed he had a previous injury that was healing; they found food in his stomach, which showed he was relaxed and not expecting to fight someone, etc.

B   Answers will vary. Possible answers:

Topic Sentence: CT scanning helped scientists learn about what might have happened to the Iceman.

Important Ideas:

The CT scan showed that he was hit from behind with an arrow. An injury on his hand was discovered to be from a few days before, so it was not likely connected to his death. The imaging also showed he had eaten a full meal before he was killed, so scientists think he was not expecting to be in danger.

REVISING PRACTICE *(page 47)*

The *Revising Practice* box contains an exercise that demonstrates several ways students can improve their first drafts.

- Allow time for students to analyze the two drafts and complete the exercise.
- Check answers as a class. Ask students to identify each change and explain how it makes the revised draft stronger.

D Revised Draft

Students should apply the revision techniques used in the *Revising Practice* box to their own drafts, where applicable.

- Explain to students that they will be using the questions as a guide for checking and improving their drafts.
- As a class, go over the questions carefully to make sure students understand them.
- Allow time for students to revise their summaries.

EDITING PRACTICE

The *Editing Practice* box trains students to spot and correct common errors related to using synonyms. As a class, go over the information in the box carefully to make sure students understand what to look out for.

- Allow students time to complete the exercise individually.
- Check answers as a class by asking students to read their corrected sentences aloud and explain the errors.

ANSWER KEY

REVISING PRACTICE

a, b, d, c

EDITING PRACTICE

1. Paraphrase: DNA is a small molecule that contains <u>information</u> for a person's cell development.

2. Paraphrase: Every individual's DNA is <u>unique</u>, so it is useful in identifying people.

3. Paraphrase: DNA phenotyping allows scientists to <u>identify</u> characteristics such as eye and hair color, the structure of faces, as well as geographic origin.

E Final Draft

Have students apply the skills taught in *Editing Practice* to their own revised drafts and check for any other errors.

- Allow time for students to edit their drafts.
- Walk around and monitor students as they work. Provide assistance as needed.
- Collect their work once they have completed it.
- For the next class, show anonymous examples of good summaries and common errors.

Ideas for … EXPANSION

Have students work in groups of three to review and edit each other's summaries further. Ask each group member to read another's summary paragraphs and try to do the following:

- Correct one error in grammar, spelling, etc.
- Give one compliment.
- Give one piece of feedback to help improve the summary.

Allow students time to read each other's summaries, take notes, and then discuss their feedback.

 UNIT REVIEW

Students can work in groups on this recap of the unit. For question **1**, encourage students to use the target vocabulary words when appropriate. For questions **2** and **3**, encourage them to check the relevant pages of the unit for answers.

- Allow students time to answer the three questions in groups.
- Ask each group to present its answer for question **1**.

CITY SOLUTIONS

ACADEMIC TRACK

Sociology / Urban Studies

ACADEMIC SKILLS

READING	Analyzing visual information
WRITING	Writing introductory and concluding paragraphs
GRAMMAR	Using the simple past and the present perfect
CRITICAL THINKING	Analyzing quotes

UNIT OVERVIEW

The theme of this unit is urban planning, and how proper planning of cities can help solve environmental problems.

- **READING 1:** Well-planned megacities, like Seoul, South Korea, can help solve the planet's many environmental issues caused by human activity.

- **VIDEO:** One company is trying to make underground farming a reality in London, in order to bring freshly grown food closer to city residents.

- **READING 2:** One architect has set out to create a database of information about different cities, and to share this information more effectively to help cities grow successfully.

Students draw on what they have read and watched to write a problem-solution essay about how a city or town overcame a problem. The unit prepares them for the writing task by introducing vocabulary to talk about urban planning and related issues, and reviewing the simple past and present perfect. It also introduces the structure of an introductory paragraph and a concluding paragraph in an essay. Finally, it takes students through the steps of brainstorming and planning, and shows them how to revise and edit their essays.

 THINK AND DISCUSS *(page 49)*

The title and questions help prepare students for the subject matter covered in the unit. The photo shows a bus stop in Curitiba, Brazil. By having bus-only lanes, the bus rapid transit system has allowed for more efficient travel in the city.

- Have students study the picture, title, and caption.

- Discuss the photo as a class. What is the most common mode of transportation in students' cities? Do they think it is convenient?

- Discuss the questions as a class. For question **1**, elicit examples of big cities in their countries. Use this as an opportunity to introduce the word *megacity* (a city with a population over 10 million). For question **2**, ask students to name a city they like and explain why. What about the city makes it special? Are there lots of places to visit? Is the transportation system reliable and easy to use? Is the city clean?

ANSWER KEY

THINK AND DISCUSS

Answers will vary. Possible answers:

1. The biggest cities in my country are New Delhi and Mumbai. They both have very big populations. So they are both very lively! Both cities are very modern in some parts, but there are also poorer areas with poor infrastructure.

2. My favorite city is Singapore. I like it because there are great parks, the public transportation is easy to use, and there is a diverse population of people from all around the world. There's also terrific food and shopping!

EXPLORE THE THEME *(pages 50–51)*

The opening spread provides information and statistics about urbanization as a growing trend.

- Allow time for students to study the spread, including the graph, and to answer the questions individually.

- Check answers as a class. Ask students why they think so many people want to live in cities.

ANSWER KEY

EXPLORE THE THEME

A Answers will vary. Possible answers:

1. More and more people are living in urban areas in all parts of the world.

2. Latin America and the Caribbean; Asia

3. Africa and Asia

B urban; growth; dense (Note: The noun *density* is used to talk about population in comparison to land space: *population density*.)

23

Reading 1

PREPARING TO READ *(page 52)*

A Building Vocabulary

The sentences are related to the theme of urbanization. They contain seven key vocabulary items that appear in the passage. Students should use contextual clues to deduce the meaning of the words.

- Have students work individually to complete the exercise.
- Check answers as a class. Elicit example sentences for each vocabulary item.

See Vocabulary Extension 3 in the Student Book for additional practice with expressions with income.

B Using Vocabulary

Students should use the new vocabulary items while discussing the questions.

- Have students work in pairs to answer the questions. If necessary, provide some prompts to help with their discussion. (1. *I'd rather live in a … because …; 2. Some aspects of city life that I like are …*)
- Check answers as a class. Elicit example answers from students.

C Predicting

In this reading passage, the title and headings provide useful insight into the passage content.

- Allow students time to skim the title and headings before answering the question.
- Discuss answers as a class. Revisit this activity after students have completed the reading.

ANSWER KEY

PREPARING TO READ

A 1. aspect

2. spread out

3. income (Note: *Income* can be hourly, daily, weekly, yearly, etc.)

4. productive

5. tend to

6. concentration (Note: Another common meaning of *concentration* is focus.)

7. suburb

B Answers will vary. Possible answers:

1. I like suburbs and rural areas because they are less crowded.

2. The aspects of city life that appeal to me include good work opportunities and easy access to public transportation. However, housing in the city is very expensive.

C Answers will vary. Correct answer: c

 1.05 Have students read the passage individually, or play the audio and have students read along.

OVERVIEW OF THE READING

The passage discusses the topic of urbanization. As the world's population is increasingly choosing to live in cities, attitudes about urban life are beginning to change. While cities used to be seen as undesirable places to live, they are now turning into a possible solution to environmental issues and global poverty. The passage discusses the benefits of urbanization. It also shares views from several experts who believe that cities can help improve shared knowledge, are better for the planet, and can help poorer countries thrive, as long as effective urban planning is a part of a city's design and growth process. The passage is based on the article *The City Solution* by Robert Kunzig, which appeared in *National Geographic* magazine.

Online search terms: The City Solution, Edward Glaeser, Stewart Brand, David Satterthwaite, Shlomo Angel

UNDERSTANDING THE READING *(pages 56–57)*

A Summarizing

Students are asked to decide which sentences belong in a summary of the reading.

- Have students work individually to complete the activity.
- Have students compare answers in pairs.
- Discuss answers as a class. Ask students why the remaining sentences are not suitable options.

B Understanding Main Ideas

Students are asked to determine the main ideas of the paragraphs in the reading.

- Have students work in pairs to complete the activity. Encourage them to skim for the topic sentence to get the main idea quickly.
- Check answers as a class. Elicit the sentences in the paragraphs that helped students identify the main ideas.

C Identifying Pros and Cons

This exercise requires students to identify examples related to positive and negative points discussed in the reading.

- Before students attempt to answer the questions, have them identify the key words they can scan for (e.g., *Glaeser*, *benefit*, etc.)
- Have students work individually to complete the activity.
- Have students compare answers in pairs.
- Discuss answers as a class. Note that in some cases, there is more than one example in the reading.

D Critical Thinking: Analyzing Quotes

The *Critical Thinking* box explains that authors may sometimes use quotes from experts as supporting details. Remind students that in Unit 1, they learned about supporting evidence in the form of examples. Quotes are another type of supporting evidence. Discuss how this kind of evidence strengthens an essay or article. For exercise **D** students are asked to read quotes from the reading passage and identify the ideas that each supports.

- Allow students time to find the quotes in the passage.
- Have them work in pairs to identify the idea supported by the quote.
- Check answers as a class. Do the students think the quotes are effective at supporting the idea(s)?

E Critical Thinking: Justifying Your Opinion

Forming your own opinions about an essay or article deepens your understanding of it. Encourage students to do this by considering what they have read about the pros and cons of urbanization, and forming their own opinions on the topic.

- Have students write down their own responses individually before discussing them in pairs.
- Discuss answers as a class. Ask for volunteers to share their opinions and the reasons for them.

ANSWER KEY

UNDERSTANDING THE READING

A 1 (See Paragraph C.); 3 (See Paragraph G.); 4 (See Paragraph H.); 6 (See Paragraph K.)

B **1.** d (Explanation: *Recent decades, however, have seen a widespread change in attitudes toward urbanization.*)

    2. b (Explanation: *This closeness reduces the cost of transporting goods, people, and ideas, and allows people to be more productive.*)

3. a (Explanation: *…cities tend to produce fewer greenhouse gas emissions per person than suburbs.*)

4. f (Explanation: *…it proves that a poor country can urbanize successfully and incredibly fast.*)

5. e (Explanation: *Some ways to densify suburbs include creating walkable town centers. … This would make people less dependent on cars.*)

6. c (Explanation: *…dense and carefully planned cities are looking more like a solution—perhaps the best hope for lifting people out of poverty without wrecking the planet.*)

C **1.** reduced cost of transporting goods, people, and ideas; easier to share information and learn from one another

2. less impact on the environment (example: half of the world's population lives on only 4 percent of land / fewer resources needed to maintain city infrastructure / city apartments use lesser energy / fewer cars)

3. managing urban growth

D **1.** Information can be shared easily in cities, allowing people to learn from one another.

2. A city's urban growth must be supported by economic development.

3. the issue of urban sprawl

4. Expanding suburban areas have led to increased energy use, air pollution, and greenhouse gas emissions.

E Answers will vary. Possible answer:

Overall, I think urbanization has a positive impact on human societies because city living is more environmentally friendly. Life is also more convenient for everyone.

 DEVELOPING READING SKILLS
(page 58)

Reading Skill: Analyzing Visual Information

The *Reading Skill* box explains how to analyze infographics—such as graphs—that accompany a reading passage. Students should first identify the kind of information that is being shown, then ask themselves how this information supports the ideas in the reading passage.

A Analyzing Visual Information

Students are asked to analyze a graph related to the content of the reading passage.

- Have students work in pairs. Tell them to look at the graph together and talk about what they see.
- Ask them to review each question and use the information in the graph to answer them. For question **3**, tell them to discuss their ideas.
- Check answers as a class. Ask students if any part of the graph was difficult to understand. If so, what could make it easier to understand?

B Analyzing Visual Information

Students are asked to analyze the diagram in Reading 1 to determine how it is connected to the content of the reading passage.

- Have students work in pairs or in small groups. Ask them to look at the diagram first before discussing their answers to questions **1–3**.
- Check answers as a class. For questions **1** and **2**, ask students which parts of the diagram gave them the answers. For question **3**, ask them what the connection between the diagram and the paragraph is.

ANSWER KEY

DEVELOPING READING SKILLS

A 1. The graph shows South Korea's economic growth from 1980 to 2015 in comparison to major European countries.

2. Paragraph F: *In the same period, South Korea has also gone from being one of the world's poorest countries to being richer than many countries in Europe.*

3. The graph provides more details about South Korea's rapid growth compared to some European countries.

B 1. The colors represent the levels of emissions—red indicates higher greenhouse gas emissions (per person), while green indicates lower emissions.

2. c

3. Paragraph D: *As a result, cities tend to produce fewer greenhouse gas emissions per person than suburbs.*

Video

VIEWING: FARMING UNDERGROUND *(pages 59–60)*

Overview of the Video

In London, a team is using hydroponic farming techniques to create the right environment underground to grow crops. This farm, set in a bomb shelter tunnel built during World War II, is powered by renewable energy. The team behind the endeavor is aiming to make urban farms a reality for cities in the near future, so that food has to travel a shorter distance to get to people's plates. Additionally, the team hopes that urban farms will help connect people living in urban areas to the origins of their food. The video is from a short clip that aired on the *National Geographic* channel.

Online search terms: Steven Dring, Richard Ballard, Growing Underground

BEFORE VIEWING

A Predicting

The photo shows entrepreneur Steven Dring in his underground farm in London. His crops are grown using hydroponic farming techniques. They receive nutrients from a nutrient solution and light from LEDs.

- Have students study the title, photo, and caption and discuss reasons for building underground farms.
- Discuss answers as a class.

B Learning About the Topic

The paragraph prepares students for the video by familiarizing them with the issues of "food miles" and how transporting food can contribute to global warming.

- Have students read the paragraph and answer the questions individually.
- Ask students to form pairs to check answers.
- Check answers as a class. For question **3**, ask students to name the countries that produced the food they recently bought. For example, ask: Where were the bananas you ate for breakfast grown? Then ask them to think about how to reduce the "food miles" of this product (e.g., by buying bananas from a local farm).

C Vocabulary in Context

This exercise introduces students to some of the key words used in the video. Students use context to deduce the meaning of the words.

- Have students work on the exercise individually.
- Ask students to form pairs to compare answers.
- Discuss as a class. Elicit example sentences for each word.

BEFORE VIEWING

A   Answers will vary. Possible answer: There's not a lot of space in cities for farming, and underground farms won't take up land that people live on.

B 1. Transporting food across long distances causes greenhouse gas emissions, which are a big contributor to global warming.

   2. "Food miles" are likely to increase as the population increases.

   3. Answers will vary. Possible answer: One way to reduce food transportation is for people to buy more food from local farmers instead of buying imported food.

C 1. distribution   **4.** carbon-neutral

   2. utilize   **5.** hydroponic farming

   3. LED

WHILE VIEWING

A ▶ Understanding Main Ideas

Have students read the items before you play the video.
- Have students complete the task while the video is playing.
- Check answers as a class.

B ▶ Understanding Details

Have students read the questions and write any answers they recall from the first viewing before playing the video a second time.
- Play the video again. Have students complete the task while the video is playing.
- Check answers as a class.

WHILE VIEWING

A   1, 3, 4, 5

B 1. F (*We are in a tunnel system that was built during the Second World War.*)

   2. T (*In London, for example, we're going to have an additional two million people in the next 10 years.*)

   3. NG

   4. T (*And so we got one bench, but when we populate it—the whole of the tunnel—we'll have a bench on the floor, bench halfway up, and a bench up here as well, so we'll be growing that.*)

AFTER VIEWING

A Reacting to the Video

Students are asked to think about why it is a problem that consumers don't know where their food is from, and how Dring's farm may help address that.
- Allow time for students to work individually to answer the questions.
- Have students share and discuss answers in pairs.
- Discuss as a class. Ask if students can suggest ways that this problem could be addressed even more fully. For example, young people could work on the farm to be a part of the food growing process.

B Critical Thinking: Evaluating

Students are asked to consider whether there are downsides to having underground farms in cities.
- Read the question aloud. Have students discuss their ideas in pairs. They should think about various aspects, such as cost, environmental issues, etc. Are there limitations to the types of farms we can have underground in cities?
- Discuss as a class.

AFTER VIEWING

A   Answers will vary. Possible answers:

   It shows that young people who grow up in cities lack an understanding of how food is actually produced. With underground farms, the food will come from a local source. If underground farms become the norm, city people will have easy access to farms and fresh food.

B   Answers will vary. Possible answers:

   If a disease breaks out at an underground farm, it's likely that many people will be affected. Another possible problem is that constructing underground farms might cost cities too much money.

Reading 2

⏱ 30 MINS **PREPARING TO READ** (page 61)

A Building Vocabulary

Students should first use a dictionary to check the definition of the words in blue before completing the sentences. Provide assistance as needed.

- Have students complete the task individually. Point out that some sentences require more than one word.
- Check answers as a class. Elicit example sentences for each vocabulary item.

B Using Vocabulary

Students should use the new vocabulary items while discussing the two questions.

- Have students work in pairs to answer the questions. If necessary, provide prompts to support their discussion. (1. *The quality of life in cities can be enhanced by …and …*; 2. *To reduce my energy consumption, I could …*)
- Check answers as a class. Elicit example answers from students.

C Predicting

Students are asked to predict how urban planner Richard Wurman studied urbanization and its effects.

- Allow time for students to write their own ideas.
- Ask them to discuss their ideas in pairs. How might this information be useful for studying urbanization?
- Discuss students' answers as a class. Revisit the activity after students have completed the reading.

ANSWER KEY

PREPARING TO READ

A **1.** safety

  2. consumption; majority

  3. phenomenon; increasingly (Note: The plural of *phenomenon* is *phenomena*.)

  4. industrial; varied

  5. basically

  6. attempt; enhance

B   Answers will vary. Possible answers:

  1. Two ways to enhance the quality of city life include making sure everyone has access to clean drinking water, and making sure the city is safe for all who live there.

  2. One thing I can do to reduce my energy consumption is to unplug my electronic devices when I am not using them.

C   Answers will vary. Correct answer:

  He collected information about the infrastructure of cities: power, water distribution, healthcare, education, etc. His work can help us understand urbanization and look at how some cities are able to grow more rapidly and/or more successfully than others.

 1.06 Have students read the passage individually, or play the audio and have students read along.

OVERVIEW OF THE READING

The reading passage features an interview with urban planner Richard Wurman. In the interview, he describes a project that he is working on to help create a better system for comparing data between cities. His hope is that making the data easier to understand will help cities learn from each other and improve their efforts to become better. The interview is an excerpt from the article *Urban Visionary* that appeared in the magazine *National Geographic Traveler*.

Online search terms: Urban Observatory, Richard Wurman, 19.20.21 Project

⏱ 60 MINS **UNDERSTANDING THE READING** (pages 65–66)

A Understanding Main Ideas

Students are asked to choose another title for the reading.

- Have students work individually to complete the activity.
- Check answers as a class. Ask students why the other options are less suitable.

B Understanding Purpose

Students are asked to match each section of the reading to its main purpose.

- Allow students time to work in pairs to complete the activity.
- Check answers as a class. Ask students where the clues were in the paragraph(s).

C Understanding Details

Students complete a concept map using details from the passage.

- Allow students time to work individually.
- Check answers as a class. Discuss where students found the relevant information.

D Inferring Meaning

Students first find and underline the words in the passage. Then they use context to deduce the meaning of the words. Lastly, they complete the definitions of the words.

- Have students work in pairs to locate the words in the passage and guess their meaning.
- Have them complete the definitions.
- Check answers as a class.

E Critical Thinking: Analyzing Visual Information

Students practice the reading skill introduced in the *Developing Reading Skills* section by answering questions about the maps in Reading 2.

- Have students work in pairs to answer the questions.
- Check answers as a class.
- Ask students to explain how the maps support content in the passage.

F Critical Thinking: Synthesizing

Students draw on information from both reading passages to match the statements to the people in the unit.

- Have students read the statements and identify the ones Wurman would agree with. Then have them refer to Reading 1 to review Glaeser's, Brand's, and Angel's opinions.
- Have students discuss their answers in pairs.
- Check answers as a class. Get volunteers to share the reasons for their answers.

Ideas for ... EXPANSION

Have students work in pairs or in small groups. Ask students to go online to browse the Urban Observatory that Wurman's team created. Tell them to launch the site app to see the data that the study has gathered. Get them to choose one "Theme" and make notes about how some cities compare in regards to this theme, according to the data on the site. Then have each group present their observations to the class.

ANSWER KEY

UNDERSTANDING THE READING

A a

B 1. a (Explanation: *The project's aim is to standardize the way information about cities … is collected and shared.*)

   2. b (Explanation: *People flock to cities because…*)

   3. e (Explanation: *There's no readily available information on the speed of growth of cities.*)

   4. d (Explanation: *So I decided to gather consistent information on 19 cities that will have more than 20 million people in the 21st century.*)

   5. c (Explanation: *…you can't solve a problem with a collection of little ideas. One has to understand them in context and in comparison to other places.*)

C 1. architect   7. urban planners

   2. urbanization   8. environmental impact

   3. business   9. 20 million

   4. media   10. resources / energy

   5. 5 years   11. online

   6. standardize

D 1. go there   4. obvious

   2. large   5. poor

   3. in comparison with

E Answers will vary. Possible answers:

   1. The maps compare the amount of green spaces in Abu Dhabi, Tokyo, and London.

   2. London (most); Abu Dhabi (least)

   3. This information might help urban planners look at ways to increase green spaces in cities.

F Answers will vary. Possible answers:

   1. Brand   3. Wurman, Glaeser

   2. Wurman   4. Angel

Writing

OVERVIEW

In this section, students learn about the introductory and concluding paragraphs of an essay. The lesson starts by reviewing the simple past and the present perfect. It then introduces the structure of and elements in the introductory and concluding paragraphs of an essay. In the *Writing Task*, students apply these lessons, along with what they learned about body paragraphs in the previous units, by writing a complete essay about an urban problem and its possible solutions. Students begin with a brainstorming exercise before selecting, organizing, and combining information in an outline. Finally, they draft their essays, improve their drafts, and correct common mistakes related to using the simple past and the present perfect.

 EXPLORING WRITTEN ENGLISH
(pages 67–69)

A Noticing

While doing this activity students should notice which verb form is used and why it is used. This exercise should be completed before going over the information in the *Language for Writing* box.

- Have students complete the activity individually. Tell them to pay close attention to the language used and what it is expressing.
- Check answers as a class. Ask students to point out the expressions that helped them decide. For example, *In 2017* in item **a** refers to a specific time.

Language for Writing: Using the Simple Past and the Present Perfect

The *Language for Writing* box reviews the use of the simple past versus the present perfect. While both are used to talk about events in the past, the simple past is used when something happened at a specified time, while the present perfect is used for something that happened at an unspecified time, or something that happened more than once in the past. Review how the present perfect is formed: *has/have* + past participle.

B Language for Writing

Students are asked to choose the correct verb form to complete the sentences.

- Have students complete the activity individually.
- Check answers as a class. Ask students the reasons for their answers.

Writing Skill: Writing an Introductory Paragraph

The first *Writing Skill* box explains the structure of the introductory paragraph and its role in the essay. It also provides information about the hook and the thesis statement—two common elements in an introduction. As the thesis statement contains the author's main message, it should highlight the main points of the essay.

C Writing Skill

Tell students to use the tips in the *Writing Skill* box to identify the best thesis statements.

- Have students work on the exercise individually.
- Have them check their answers in pairs.
- Discuss students' answers as a class, going over again what makes a strong thesis statement. Note that the thesis statement should let the reader know what to expect later in the essay.

D Writing Skill

Students evaluate the hooks and choose the better one for each topic. Tell students to use the tips in the *Writing Skill* box to help them.

- Have students work on the exercise individually.
- Have them check their answers in pairs.
- Discuss students' answers as a class, reviewing what makes a good hook: a surprising fact, an interesting question, or an imaginary situation related to the topic.

E Writing Skill

Students match the topics in exercise **D** with an appropriate thesis statement.

- Have students work on the exercise individually.
- Have them check their answers in pairs.
- Discuss students' answers as a class.

Writing Skill: Writing a Concluding Paragraph

The second *Writing Skill* box introduces the elements of a concluding paragraph. In addition to summarizing the thesis, a concluding paragraph often leaves the reader with a final thought. Some ways of writing a final thought include asking a question or making a prediction.

F Writing Skill

Students write a summary statement for each thesis statement in exercise **E**. Explain that students should rewrite each statement in their own words. Tell students to use the tips in the second *Writing Skill* box to help them.

- Review the three paraphrasing techniques that students learned in Unit 2: using synonyms, changing parts of speech, and combining information.
- Have students work on the exercise individually.
- Have them share their answers in pairs.
- Discuss as a class. Ask volunteers to share their summary statements.

G Writing Skill

Students write a final thought for a summary statement from exercise **F**. Tell students to use the tips in the second *Writing Skill* box to help them.

- If needed, review the options introduced in the second *Writing Skill* box for writing a final thought (making a prediction, asking a question).
- Have students work on the exercise individually.
- Have them compare their answers in pairs.
- Discuss students' answers as a class. Ask volunteers to share their final thoughts.

WRITING TASK *(page 70)*

A Brainstorming

Read the *Goal* box aloud so students are familiar with the writing task before brainstorming. The aim is to write an essay about a problem in a city or town. The essay should also present one thing that was done to solve the problem. When brainstorming, the first step is to list as many ideas as possible without worrying too much about how good the ideas are, as long as they are on topic.

- Encourage students to choose a city or town that they know well. Allow them time to do research online to collect information, if necessary. (Note that students will be guided further in Unit 8 on how to find reliable sources online.)
- Allow time for students to work individually and note their ideas.
- Have them discuss their ideas in pairs and give each other feedback.

B Planning

After brainstorming, the next steps involve selecting the best ideas, organizing the information, and writing the thesis statement. Remind students that complete sentences are not necessary for the supporting details. It is more important to focus on organizing their information. Point out that students will also note their ideas for the introductory and concluding paragraphs.

- Allow time for students to complete their outlines individually. Provide assistance as needed.

C First Draft

- Have students write a first draft of their essay based on their outline.
- Allow time for students to complete the task individually. Provide assistance as needed. Refrain from error correction at this point.

ANSWER KEY

WRITING TASK

A Answers will vary. Possible answer:

City: San Francisco; Improvements: removed Embarcadero Bridge, renovated the waterfront area, etc.

B Answers will vary. Possible answer:

Introductory Paragraph

Hook: Imagine your shock when you visit San Francisco for the first time, and you have to walk under an ugly freeway to get to the bay.

Thesis Statement: However, one improvement that has made the city a more beautiful place for residents and tourists is tearing down the Embarcadero Freeway.

Concluding Paragraph

Summary Statement: The removal of the Embarcadero Freeway has made the waterfront area attractive and accessible to both visitors and San Franciscans.

Final Thought: What other improvements might make the city an even more beautiful place to live and visit?

REVISING PRACTICE *(page 71)*

The *Revising Practice* box contains an exercise that demonstrates several ways students can improve their first drafts.

- Allow students time to analyze the essay draft and complete the exercise.
- Check answers as a class. Ask students to identify each change that was made and explain how it makes the revised draft stronger.

D Revised Draft

Students should apply the revision techniques used in the *Revising Practice* box to their own drafts, where applicable.

- Explain to students that they will be using the questions as a guide for checking and improving their drafts.
- As a class, go over the questions carefully to make sure students understand them.
- Allow students time to revise their essays.

EDITING PRACTICE

The *Editing Practice* box trains students to spot and correct common errors related to the present perfect tense. As a class, review the information in the box carefully to make sure students understand what to look out for.

- Allow students time to complete the exercise individually.
- Check answers as a class by asking students to read their corrected sentences aloud and explain the errors.

ANSWER KEY

REVISING PRACTICE

1. c, a, b
2. **d.** Sentence to cross out: Visitors can take ferries to Alcatraz and take a tour of the old prison.

   e. Walking under the freeway <u>was not</u> a pleasant experience.

   f. In 1989, part of the freeway <u>was</u> destroyed by an earthquake …

EDITING PRACTICE

1. The city <u>has</u> made a lot of changes over the past 10 years.
2. Residents have <u>enjoyed</u> the renovations to the city center and the public parks.
3. The new subway system has <u>made</u> it easier to get across town.
4. It is now safer for people to ride their bikes to work because the government has <u>added</u> bicycle lanes to busy streets.
5. San Francisco city planners <u>have</u> created a beautiful walkable area alongside the bay.

E Final Draft

Have students apply the skills taught in *Editing Practice* to their own revised drafts and check for any other errors.

- Allow time for students to edit their drafts.
- Walk around and monitor students as they work. Provide assistance as needed.
- Collect students' work once they have completed it.
- For the next class, show anonymous examples of good essays and common errors.

🕙 10 MINS UNIT REVIEW

Students can work in groups on this recap of the unit. For question **1**, encourage students to use the target vocabulary words when appropriate. For questions **2** and **3**, encourage them to check the relevant pages of the unit for answers.

- Allow students time to answer the questions in groups.
- Ask each group to present its answer for question **1**.

DANGER ZONES

ACADEMIC TRACK
Earth Science

ACADEMIC SKILLS
READING	Understanding referencing and cohesion
WRITING	Writing a process essay
GRAMMAR	Using parallel structures
CRITICAL THINKING	Inferring

UNIT OVERVIEW
The theme of this unit is natural disasters, and how some regions of the world are more susceptible to them. From earthquakes to volcanic eruptions to hurricanes, vulnerable areas can be changed in a moment when catastrophe strikes.

- **READING 1:** Scientists are studying whether animals can sense natural disasters by observing their behavior. If proven true, it may be an effective and inexpensive way to predict natural disasters.

- **VIDEO:** Hurricanes are monster storms that cost lives and devastate vulnerable areas; scientists are trying to find ways to better predict a hurricane's movement.

- **READING 2:** Yellowstone National Park sits on top of a supervolcano, and an eruption could change the face of the planet.

Students draw on what they have read and watched to write an essay about a natural hazard and how to prepare for it. The unit prepares them for the writing task by introducing vocabulary to talk about disasters, along with how to use parallel nouns, verbs, and adjectives. It also introduces process essays and some transition words and phrases that can be used in such essays. It then takes students through the steps of brainstorming, planning, revising, and editing their essays.

 THINK AND DISCUSS *(page 73)*

The photo shows the landscape around Mount Sinabung, an active volcano in Sumatra, Indonesia. The volcano had been dormant for centuries before starting to erupt in 2010. The title and questions help prepare students for the subject matter covered in the unit.

- Have students study the picture, title, and caption. Elicit the meaning of *zone* (an area, usually one that shares a common characteristic, such as a *car-free zone* of a city).
- Discuss the photo as a class. What kind of contrast is shown in the photo? (beautiful natural area with a smoking, dangerous volcano)
- Discuss the two questions as a class. For question **1**, have the class brainstorm a list of natural disasters. Create a mind map on the board and review the meaning of each word. For question **2**, ask students to think back to what they learned in Unit 3 about urban planning. Can better urban and town planning also help make natural disasters less devastating? If so, how?

ANSWER KEY

THINK AND DISCUSS

Answers will vary. Possible answers:

1. cyclones, tsunamis, floods, earthquakes, volcanic eruptions, sinkholes, forest fires, etc.

2. Although some places are at risk of being affected by extreme natural events, they often have positive sides, too. A coastal area, for example, may face risk of storms or tsunamis, but is also beautiful and a good place for water sports.

EXPLORE THE THEME (pages 74–75)

The opening spread contains an infographic that shows vulnerable areas around the world, and the kinds of natural disasters that affect these areas. It also explains that the damage cost of natural disasters in these areas is very high.

- Allow time for students to study the spread and answer the questions individually.
- Check answers as a class.

ANSWER KEY

EXPLORE THE THEME

A 1. Earthquakes: the west coasts of North and South America, as well as in Japan, New Zealand, and parts of China.

Volcanoes: Central and South America, Indonesia, and Japan.

Cyclones: Asia, Madagascar, and the east coast of North America.

2. They are in highly populated areas.

B hazard; throughout; disaster

Ideas for … EXPANSION

Have students work in small groups to talk about natural disasters that are common in their countries. If students live in a vulnerable area, ask them to talk about what people do to prepare for the type of disaster that is common there. Have they prepared any kind of emergency pack at home? Do they have a plan ready to follow if a disaster strikes? Note that students will be asked to write on a similar topic at the end of the unit. This discussion can provide a useful brainstorming session for students to refer back to before they write.

Reading 1

PREPARING TO READ (page 76)

A Building Vocabulary

The paragraph is related to the reading passage. It describes attempts to make an early-warning system for earthquakes. It contains seven vocabulary words that are used in the passage. Students should use context to deduce the meaning of the words.

- Have students work individually to complete the exercise.
- Check answers as a class. Elicit example sentences for each vocabulary item.

See Vocabulary Extension 4 in the Student Book for additional practice with changing nouns/adjectives into verbs with the suffix -en.

B Using Vocabulary

Students should use the new vocabulary items while discussing the two questions.

- Have students work in pairs to answer the questions.
- Check answers as a class. Elicit example answers from students. For question **2**, ask students if they think the alert method is effective.

C Brainstorming

Students should work in pairs to think of as many ideas as possible. Offer students one or two examples before they begin. (Examples: check satellite imagery for weather; check data on seismic activity)

- Allow students time to brainstorm ideas in pairs.
- Discuss ideas as a class. Create a mind map on the board using students' responses.

D Predicting

If necessary, review how to use skimming to read quickly for comprehension: students should read the first and last sentences and quickly go over the sentences in between, focusing only on the content words.

- Allow students time to skim the first two paragraphs.
- Get them to write two ideas in response to the question.
- Discuss answers as a class. Revisit this exercise after students have completed the reading.

PREPARING TO READ

A 1. alert

2. forecast

3. destruction

4. get out

5. affordable

6. effectively

7. deadly

B Answers will vary. Possible answers:

1. hurricanes, earthquakes, tsunamis, tornadoes, floods, heat waves, avalanches, blizzards, etc.

2. The most common natural hazards we experience in my country are earthquakes. People are alerted by an alarm on their cell phones that goes off one minute before a large earthquake is expected.

C Answers will vary. Possible answers:

Scientists look at seismic data to predict earthquakes. For weather-related disasters, they watch meteorological reports.

D Answers will vary. Correct answers:

Scientists think that atmospheric changes affect animals' serotonin levels, causing them to feel restless and leave an area. Scientists think that birds can hear the infrasound produced by an oncoming storm, which keeps them from going where the storm is about to hit.

🎧 **1.07** Have students read the passage individually, or play the audio and have students read along.

OVERVIEW OF THE READING

The passage describes how animals have been observed leaving places before a large natural disaster strikes and discusses the possibility of using animals to forecast deadly disasters. Some scientists believe that certain animals may be sensitive to atmospheric changes that happen before earthquakes. They also think that birds may be able to hear infrasound from a big storm. The passage content is based on two articles that appeared on *National Geographic*: *Scientists Seek Foolproof Signal to Predict Earthquakes* by Richard Lovett and *Birds May Have Sensed Severe Storm Days in Advance* by Carrie Arnold.

Online search terms: Scientists Seek Foolproof Signal to Predict Earthquakes, Birds May Have Sensed Severe Storm Days in Advance, Rachel Grant, Gunnar Kramer

UNDERSTANDING THE READING
(pages 80–81)

A Summarizing

Students are asked to complete a summary of the reading.

- Have students work individually to complete the activity. Point out that each space should only contain one word, but there is more than one answer choice for some questions.
- Get students to form pairs to compare answers.
- Discuss answers as a class.

B Understanding a Process

Students are asked to identify the steps in the process of how scientists think animals are alerted to a upcoming danger before fleeing an area.

- Have students work individually to complete the activity.
- Check answers as a class. Ask where students found the relevant information. (Paragraph F)

C Understanding Main Ideas

Students answer questions about key information in Paragraphs H–K.

- Have students read the questions first before scanning the passage for answers.
- Allow them time to complete the activity individually.
- Check answers as a class. Ask students where they found the answers.

D Understanding Details

Students test their understanding of the details in the passage by answering with true, false, or not given. Note that the questions refer only to information in Paragraphs C–G.

- Have students work individually to complete the activity.
- Ask students to form pairs to compare answers.
- Discuss answers as a class. Elicit where in the reading students found the details, and discuss how to make any false statement true.

E Inferring Meaning

Students first find and underline the words in the passage. Then they use context to deduce the meaning of the words. Lastly, they match the words to their definitions.

- Have students work in pairs to locate the words in the passage and deduce their meaning.
- Have them complete the exercise by matching the words to their definitions.
- Check answers as a class.

F Critical Thinking: Inferring

The *Critical Thinking* box explains how to infer in order to understand unstated information in a passage. Readers draw conclusions based on what is implied from the information given. For exercise **F**, students are asked to reread Paragraph I and identify information that can be inferred from the paragraph.

- Allow students time to read the paragraph and choose the two statements.
- Have students form pairs to compare their answers, sharing why they were able to make those inferences.
- Check answers as a class. Elicit reasons why each statement can or cannot be inferred.

DEVELOPING READING SKILLS
(page 82)

Reading Skill: Understanding Referencing and Cohesion

The *Reading Skill* box explains how to use referents to refer to an antecedent (an idea that appeared earlier in the text). Some referents introduced are: pronouns (*I*, *you*, *we*, *they*, etc.), possessive adjectives (*my*, *your*, *our*, *its*, etc.), and demonstrative pronouns (*that*, *this*, *these*, *those*).

A Understanding Referencing

Students are asked to identify the antecedents for each referent.

- Allow students time to read the sentences and complete the exercise individually.
- Ask students to form pairs to compare answers.
- Check answers as a class.

B Understanding Referencing

Students are asked to identify the antecedents for each referent in a paragraph from the passage.

- Allow students time to read the paragraph and complete the exercise individually.
- Ask students to form pairs to compare answers.
- Check answers as a class.

Video

40 MINS **VIEWING: HURRICANES**
(pages 83–84)

Overview of the Video

The video provides more information about hurricanes, (also called typhoons or cyclones). These violent storms can be over 500 miles (805 km) wide with winds up to 200 miles (322 km) per hour. When they make landfall, the damage and destruction can be devastating. One of the most dangerous parts of a hurricane is the storm surge, a wall of water that overcomes a coastal area when a hurricane hits. Scientists are using technology to try to better predict the directions that these monster storms may take, so fewer lives will be lost to them. This video originally appeared on *National Geographic* as *Hurricanes 101*.

Online search terms: Hurricanes 101, Watch Daredevils Fly Into a Hurricane for Science

BEFORE VIEWING

A Predicting

The photo shows residents being evacuated from an area affected by Hurricane Harvey, one of the costliest hurricanes to affect the United States.
- Have students study the title, photo, and caption for the video and predict what they may see.
- Ask students to draw from any background knowledge or personal experience they have had with large storms to answer the question.
- Discuss as a class.

B Learning About the Topic

The paragraph prepares students for the video by providing information about how a hurricane causes damage. Students use their own words to complete sentences that explain terms related to hurricanes.
- Have students read the paragraph and complete the sentences individually.
- Have them compare answers in pairs.
- Check answers as a class. Ask students if they have ever experienced a hurricane, typhoon, or cyclone. (Note that these storms have different names based on where they occur—otherwise they are the same kind of storm.)

C Vocabulary in Context

This exercise introduces students to some of the key words used in the video. Students use context to deduce the meaning of the words.
- Have students work on the exercise individually.
- Ask students to form pairs to check answers.
- Discuss answers as a class. Elicit example sentences for each word.

ANSWER KEY

BEFORE VIEWING

A   Answers will vary. Possible answers:

Hurricanes can cause bad flooding. The strong winds in hurricanes can destroy buildings.

B   Answers will vary. Possible answers:

1. A storm surge is the large amount of water that rushes over the land during a hurricane.

2. To make landfall is to come on to the land from the ocean.

3. Debris is material from structures and other things that have been destroyed during the storm.

C 1. moist

2. catastrophic (Note: The noun *catastrophe* is also commonly used when talking about natural disasters.)

3. diameter

WHILE VIEWING

A ▶ Understanding Main Ideas

Have students read the items before playing the video. Note that there are three extra items.
- Have students complete the task while the video is playing.
- Check answers as a class.

B ▶ Understanding Details

Have students read the questions and write any answers they recall from the first viewing before playing the video a second time.
- Play the video again. Have students complete the task while the video is playing.
- Check answers as a class. Ask students if they think a hurricane hunter's job is more interesting or dangerous. Would they want to do it?

AFTER VIEWING

A Reacting to the Video

Students are asked to reflect on their knowledge of hurricane-related news. Note that hurricanes are also known as typhoons and cyclones, depending on where they occur.

- Have students work in pairs. Tell them to share any news or stories about recent big storms that they have heard about.
- Have students share with the class what their group discussed.

B Critical Thinking: Applying

Students draw on information from both Reading 1 and the video to formulate their answers.

- Read the questions aloud. Have students discuss their ideas in pairs or small groups. Get them to also give reasons for their responses.
- If time permits, discuss as a class.

Reading 2

PREPARING TO READ   *(page 85)*

30 MINS

A Building Vocabulary

Students should first use dictionaries to check the definition of the words in blue before using them to complete the sentences. Students should change the form of the words as needed.

- Have students complete the task individually.
- Check answers as a class. Elicit example sentences for each vocabulary item.

B Using Vocabulary

Students should use the new vocabulary items while discussing the questions.

- Have students work in pairs to answer the questions. If necessary, provide prompts to support their discussion.
- Discuss as a class. Elicit example responses from students.

C Brainstorming

Students are asked to infer what a supervolcano is like compared to a volcano.

- Ask students to form pairs to share their ideas.
- Discuss as a class. Ask for volunteers to share their ideas.

D Predicting

Students are asked to look at the photos and headings to predict topics that are covered in the passage.

- Allow time for students to skim the headings and look at the pictures.
- Discuss answers as a class. Revisit this exercise after students have completed the reading.

B Answers will vary. Possible answers:

I watched a volcanic eruption on a TV program once. Some volcanic eruptions I've heard of are Eyjafjallajökull in Iceland, Mount Vesuvius in Italy, Krakatoa in Indonesia, and Mount St. Helens in the United States.

C Predictions will vary. Correct answer:

A supervolcano is bigger and more powerful than a regular volcano.

D Predictions will vary. Correct answer:

1, 2, 4

🔊 **1.08** Have students read the passage individually, or play the audio and have students read along.

OVERVIEW OF THE READING

Yellowstone National Park in the United States sits on top of a supervolcano—a volcano so powerful that if it erupts, it would change the planet's landscape dramatically and cause entire species to go extinct. In the 2.1 million years since this supervolcano formed, scientists believe that it has erupted three times. The giant caldera crater in Yellowstone is evidence of the last eruption 640,000 years ago. This eruption carried ash as far south as the Gulf of Mexico. The land above the caldera has been experiencing periods of rising and falling for the last 15,000 years, which means an eruption is likely at some point, but scientists are unable to predict exactly when that will happen. The passage is based on content in the *National Geographic* article *When Yellowstone Explodes* by Joel Achenbach.

Online search terms: Yellowstone supervolcano, When Yellowstone Explodes

 UNDERSTANDING THE READING
(pages 91–92)

A Summarizing

Students complete a summary of the passage using suitable words. Note that in some cases, more than one answer is possible.

- Have students work individually to complete the summary.
- Check answers as a class. Elicit any alternative answers where appropriate (for example, item **1** could be *bigger* or *larger*).

B Understanding Visual Information

Students answer questions about the infographic on the final page of the reading passage.

- Complete the first question with the whole class as an example.
- Allow students time to work individually.
- Check answers as a class. Discuss where students found the relevant information.

C Critical Thinking: Inferring

Students reread Paragraphs C and D and decide which of the statements can be inferred based on the information in the passage. Students are practicing the critical thinking skill introduced in the *Understanding the Reading* section of Reading 1.

- Allow students time to reread the paragraphs and choose the two statements.
- Have them form pairs to compare their answers, explaining how they were able to make those inferences.
- Check answers as a class. Elicit reasons why each statement can or cannot be inferred from the passage.

D Understanding a Process

Students use information in Paragraph B to put the stages of a super-eruption in the correct order.

- Have students work individually to complete the exercise.
- Check answers as a class.

E Inferring Meaning

Students first find and underline the words in the passage. Then they use context to deduce the meaning of the words. Lastly, they complete the definitions of the words.

- Have students work in pairs to locate the words in the passage and deduce their meaning.
- Have them complete the exercise.
- Check answers as a class.

F Critical Thinking: Analyzing Evidence

Students scan the passage to find evidence of the supervolcano's existence and reasons for the uncertainty of its eruption cycle.

- Have students work in pairs to look at the relevant parts of the reading and find the answers.
- Check answers as a class.

Ideas for ... EXPANSION

Get students to work in small groups to learn about another supervolcano. Have them do research online to find out some basic background information about the supervolcano such as its history of eruptions, as well as any other interesting facts. An example of another supervolcano is Lake Toba in Indonesia. Tell groups to make a poster to introduce their supervolcano to the class. Have each group give a short presentation about their supervolcano using their poster.

ANSWER KEY

UNDERSTANDING THE READING

A **1.** bigger / larger

    2. more powerful

    3. Yellowstone National Park

    4. 2.1 million years

    5. super-eruptions

    6. sunlight / the sun

    7. to fall / to decrease / to drop

    8. 15,000

B **1.** b (Explanation: The graphic compares the supervolcano eruptions in Yellowstone to the Mount St. Helens eruption in 1980.)

    2. 240 cubic miles of debris

    3. the third eruption

    4. Paragraphs C and D

C 2, 3

D b, f, e, d, c, a (See Paragraph B.)

E **1.** large

    2. understand

    3. section

    4. several times

F **1.** a crater surrounded by mountains; a thick layer of heated, compacted ash; the land near the caldera is actively rising and falling

    2. Scientists are not certain what is happening under the caldera's surface. / Scientists have only been keeping records since the 1970s, so it's hard to draw conclusions. / The caldera is going through a rise-and-fall cycle, but scientists don't know when the cycles will cause a super-eruption.

Writing

OVERVIEW

In this section, students learn about writing a process essay. The lesson starts by teaching students how to use parallel structures in a sentence, and then goes on to introduce the organization of a process essay. In the *Writing Task*, students apply these lessons by writing an essay about how to prepare for a particular natural hazard. Students begin the task with a brainstorming exercise, before selecting and organizing the related information in an outline. Students then draft their essays, revise their drafts, and correct common mistakes related to the use of parallel structures.

 EXPLORING WRITTEN ENGLISH
(pages 93–95)

A Noticing

Students should notice the parallel structures in the sentences as they examine the underlined words. This exercise is to be done before going over the information in the *Language for Writing* box.

- Have students complete the task in pairs. Tell them to pay close attention to the language and to share what they notice about it. Do the first one as an example, if needed.
- Discuss as a class. Ask students to point out the similarities they noticed in each sentence.

Language For Writing: Using Parallel Structures

The *Language for Writing* box introduces the requirement for grammatical consistency when you have two ideas of equal importance in a sentence. Parallel nouns, verbs, and adjectives should be joined by *and* or *or* in a sentence and have the same grammatical form. Parallel structures can be used at the word, phrase, or clause level.

B Language for Writing

Students practice combining sentences with parallel ideas. They may need to change the form of the ideas presented to create the parallel structures.

- Have students complete the activity individually.
- Get them to share their answers in pairs.
- Check answers as a class.

Writing Skill: Writing a Process Essay

The *Writing Skill* box introduces the structure and organization of a process essay. In a process essay, the goal is to explain how to do something, and the body paragraphs introduce the steps either in chronological order or order of importance. A topic sentence in a process essay should state the step or steps that the paragraph focuses on, while the supporting details that follow should help the reader better understand the process.

C Writing Skill

Students put the steps of a process in a suitable order, before using the steps to write a process paragraph. Tell students to refer to the tips and phrases in the *Writing Skill* box for support.

- Have students work on the exercise individually.
- Have them form pairs to check their answers.
- Discuss as a class. Was their paragraph similar to their partner's? Did they use different transition words? Point out that variety in word choice is good, and helps a writer develop their own voice.

D Writing Skill

Students pick one step from exercise **C** to practice brainstorming ideas for supporting details for a process paragraph.

- Allow students time to work on the exercise individually. Tell them to choose any step that they think they could add more ideas to. Point out that they are only writing notes, not full sentences.
- Have them form pairs to share their ideas. Ask partners to offer feedback or give additional ideas.

E Writing Skill

Students use their brainstorming notes from exercise **D** to write complete sentences.

- Have students work on the exercise individually.
- Have them share their sentences with a partner. Tell students to offer each other feedback.
- Discuss as a class. Ask for volunteers to share their entire writing process from exercises **D** and **E**. Which step did they choose? What notes did they brainstorm? And what sentences did they come up with?

ANSWER KEY

WRITING SKILL

C   Answers will vary. Possible answer:

6, 5, 2, 3, 1, 4

I'm planning for a vacation. First, I need to choose a place to go. Second, I have to search and reserve flights and hotels. Before packing my bags, I have to check the weather. Lastly, I will download movies or shows to watch on the flight.

D   Answers will vary. Possible answer:

Step: Pack your bags.

get luggage out of closet; choose clothes suitable for the beach and water sports; warm clothes for plane ride home; pack toiletries, etc.

E   Answers will vary. Possible answer:

After checking the weather, I need to pack my bags. To do that, first I have to get my suitcase out of the closet. Then I need to choose clothes that are suitable to wear at the beach and for water sports. I also need to pack some warm clothes for cold weather when I return. Another important thing is to pack toiletries.

WRITING TASK *(page 96)*

A Brainstorming

Read the *Goal* box aloud so students are familiar with the writing task before brainstorming. The aim is to explain the steps of preparing for a natural hazard. When brainstorming, students should list as many ideas as possible. Ideas should be briefly worded. They need not be listed in any order.

- Explain that students can choose a natural disaster that they read about in the unit, or another one that they are familiar with.
- Tell students to start by listing the risks and the possible effects of the natural hazard, and then thinking about how to prepare for them. Remind them that short answers are acceptable.
- Allow students time to work individually and write their ideas.
- Have them discuss their ideas in pairs.

B Planning

Students complete the outline by noting the two most important preparation methods in their body paragraphs. They also make notes for their introductory and concluding paragraphs. Remind students that complete sentences are not necessary for the details. It is more important to focus on organizing their information.

- Allow time for students to complete their outlines individually. Provide assistance as needed.
- Encourage students to note transition words from the *Writing Skill* box that will be useful to connect ideas.

C First Draft

Have students write a first draft of their essay based on their outline.

- Allow time for students to complete the task individually. Provide assistance as needed. Refrain from error correction at this point.

WRITING TASK

A Answers will vary. Possible answer:

Natural hazard: earthquake

Risks: things fall over in homes, water stops working, need to evacuate, etc.

Ideas for preparation: keep heavy or dangerous items off of high shelves; have bottled water in house; pack an emergency evacuation bag, etc.

B Answers will vary. Possible answer:

Thesis Statement: To prepare for a large earthquake, residents should pack emergency supplies and secure any household items that could fall or cause injuries.

Body Paragraphs

Topic Sentence 1: First, make your home less dangerous by moving household items around.

Details: take heavy stuff off from high shelves; make sure high items are secured to walls; don't sleep near things that can fall down on you, etc.

Topic Sentence 2: Second, preparing an evacuation plan ahead of time will make getting to a safe place quicker in an emergency situation.

Details: pack an emergency bag with essentials; store extra shoes in an accessible place; have everyone in the family agree on a place to meet if separated, etc.

Concluding Paragraph

Summary Statement: By being prepared for an evacuation and making your home as safe as possible, residents can increase their chance of survival.

Final Thought: We may not be able to accurately predict earthquakes yet, but we should at least be prepared for them.

REVISING PRACTICE *(page 97)*

The *Revising Practice* box contains an exercise that demonstrates several ways students can improve their first draft.

- Allow time for students to analyze the draft and complete the exercise.
- Check answers as a class. Ask students to identify each change and explain how it makes the revised draft stronger.

D Revised Draft

Students should apply the revision techniques used in the *Revising Practice* box to their own drafts, where applicable.

- Explain to students that they will be using the questions as a guide for checking and improving their drafts.
- As a class, go over the questions carefully to make sure students understand them.
- Allow time for students to revise their essays.

EDITING PRACTICE

The *Editing Practice* box trains students to spot and correct common errors related to parallel structures. As a class, go over the information in the box carefully to make sure students understand what to look out for.

- Allow time for students to complete the exercise individually.
- Check answers as a class by asking students to read out their corrected sentences and explain the errors.

REVISING PRACTICE

1. c, a, b
2. **d.** Sentence to cross out: The best places to look for cheap flights and hotel rooms are discount travel websites.

   e. First importantly → Most importantly

   f. Travelers should also … and <u>keep</u> copies in different parts of their luggage.

EDITING PRACTICE

1. People can prepare for fires by creating an escape plan and <u>discussing</u> it with family members.
2. Keep important papers <u>and medicines</u> in one place.
3. If you need to take pets with you, pet carriers <u>and extra pet food</u> are important to have.
4. <u>Walk</u> around your house and identify things you will need to take.
5. Pack a bag with clothes <u>and necessities</u> for each family member.

E Final Draft

Have students apply the skills taught in *Editing Practice* to their own revised drafts and check for any other errors.

- Allow time for students to edit their drafts.
- Walk around and monitor students as they work. Provide assistance as needed.
- Collect their work once they have completed it.
- For the next class, show anonymous examples of good essays and common errors.

Ideas for … EXPANSION

Have students work in groups of three to help review and edit each other's essays further. Ask each student to read another group member's essay and do the following:

- Correct one error in grammar, spelling, etc.
- Give one compliment.
- Give one piece of feedback to help improve the essay.

Allow students time to read each other's essays, take notes, and then discuss their feedback.

UNIT REVIEW

Students can work in groups on this recap of the unit. For question **1**, encourage students to use the target vocabulary words when appropriate. For questions **2** and **3**, encourage them to check the relevant pages of the unit for answers.

- Allow students time to answer the three questions in groups.
- Ask each group to present its answer for question **1**.

THE TRAVEL BUSINESS

5

ACADEMIC TRACK
Economics / Business

ACADEMIC SKILLS
READING	Analyzing causes and effects
WRITING	Writing a cause-effect essay
GRAMMAR	Using *if* ... , *(then)* ...
CRITICAL THINKING	Evaluating arguments

UNIT OVERVIEW

This unit focuses on efforts being made by the tourism industry to have a less negative impact on vacation destinations. While tourism is a source of income for the travel destinations, it can often harm natural places in the long term if care is not taken. The unit also introduces alternative kinds of travel, in particular geotourism and ecotourism, which aim to have a positive impact on local people and benefit travelers by offering deeper insights into the culture and history of a place.

- **READING 1:** In an interview, an advocate of geotourism explains the benefits of this new tourism approach.

- **VIDEO:** The Galápagos Islands offer an example of how tourism may negatively affect a place of natural beauty, as well as how a country and community are now working to reduce the problem.

- **READING 2:** Examples of successful ecotourism businesses are introduced in Ecuador, Nepal, and Australia.

Students draw on what they have read and watched to write a cause-effect essay on the negative or positive effects of tourism in a specific location. The unit prepares them for the writing task by introducing vocabulary for talking about tourism, and words and phrases that signal cause-effect relationships. It also teaches students how to use an *if*-clause to express cause and effect and introduces the elements in a cause-effect essay. Finally, it takes students through the steps of brainstorming, planning, revising, and editing their essays.

 THINK AND DISCUSS *(page 99)*

The photo shows Sheikh Zayed Grand Mosque, one of the largest mosques in the world. The title and questions help prepare students for the subject matter covered in the unit. Students will learn in the *Explore the Theme* section that tourism in Abu Dhabi is growing at a fast pace.

- Have students study the picture, title, and caption. Elicit ideas about the meaning of *the travel business* (it refers to the tourism industry).
- Discuss the photo as a class. Are there any famous sites that get many visitors every year in students' countries?
- Discuss the two questions as a class. For question **1**, encourage students to consider what they have learned in earlier units in regard to urban life when discussing possible positive impacts of tourism. For question **2**, ask students to think about various aspects such as local culture and the environment.

ANSWER KEY

THINK AND DISCUSS

Answers will vary. Possible answers:

1. Tourism can bring a lot of money into a city, which can then be used to improve the city and its services.

2. Tourism can cause overdevelopment in rural areas as towns or small cities build places to accommodate tourists. Natural areas may be destroyed in the process of this development.

EXPLORE THE THEME *(pages 100–101)*

15 MINS

The opening spread provides information about trends in global travel, such as the top destinations and the fastest-growing destination cities. Bangkok was the most popular destination in 2016, and the top-three fastest-growing cities for visitors are in Japan, China, and the United Arab Emirates.

- Allow time for students to study the spread and answer the questions individually.
- Check answers as a class. As the class discusses question **2**, revisit the *Think and Discuss* question **1** as well. Are their answers still the same?
- Elicit example sentences from students for each of the yellow words.

Ideas for … EXPANSION

Have students work in groups to discuss attitudes toward tourists in their cities. Do many tourists visit their cities? Do they think tourism is beneficial for their cities? Why or why not?

ANSWER KEY

EXPLORE THE THEME

A   Answers will vary. Possible answer:

1. I think the cities all have fantastic food, really interesting culture, and great shopping. Many people also travel there for business.
2. Mass tourism injects a lot of money into a local economy, which in turn can be used to make the infrastructure of a city or town better for its residents and visitors.

B   maintain; economy; distinctive (Note that it is easy to mix up the adjectives *distinctive* and *distinct* because they are used in rather similar ways. Something that is *distinctive* has a quality that makes it stand out from others, whereas *distinct* is used to describe something that is separate or different.)

Reading 1

30 MINS

PREPARING TO READ *(page 102)*

A Building Vocabulary

The paragraph is about alternative forms of tourism, which is part of the focus of the passage. Students should use context to deduce the meaning of the words in blue and match them to their definitions.

- Have students work individually to complete the exercise.
- Check answers as a class. Elicit example sentences for each vocabulary item.

B Building Vocabulary

Students use the context of the sentences to deduce the meaning of the words in blue.

- Have students work individually to complete the exercise.
- Check answers as a class. Elicit example sentences for each vocabulary item.

See Vocabulary Extension 5 in the Student Book for additional practice with adjectives and nouns ending in -ive.

C Using Vocabulary

Students should use the new vocabulary items while discussing the two questions.

- Have students work in pairs to answer the questions. If necessary, provide some prompts to help with the discussion.
- Check answers as a class. Elicit example answers from students.

D Brainstorming

Students prepare for the reading passage by thinking about the effects of mass tourism.

- Ask them to think about the question before discussing in pairs.
- Allow pairs time to share and discuss their answers.
- Discuss answers as a class. Elicit opinions and ideas from each pair.

E Predicting

Students read the first paragraph and predict how geotourism differs from mass tourism.

- Allow students time to read the first paragraph.
- Have students form pairs to discuss the question and list the differences.
- Discuss as a class. Get volunteers to share their ideas. Revisit this exercise after students have completed the entire reading.

PREPARING TO READ

A 1. earn a living

2. partnership

3. alternative

B 1. b

2. a

3. a

4. b

C Answers will vary. Possible answers:

1. I am from Hokkaido, Japan. Tourists come to Hokkaido to ski in winter, but actually I think our most distinctive attraction is our many flower fields in summer. There aren't many open, flat places in Japan, so Hokkaido offers a unique experience.

2. My city government preserved a historic post office by turning it into a museum.

D Answers will vary. Possible answers:

Positive effects: The money that people pay for their tours may help protect the natural areas; People learn about why it is important to protect a natural place and help spread the word, etc.

Negative effects: Tourists may damage a place, even if not intentionally. So mass tourism can harm an ecosystem; Too many people in a natural place takes away from its beauty and specialness, etc.

E Answers will vary. Correct answer: Geotourism aims to preserve the geographic character of a place.

🎧 **1.09** Have students read the passage individually, or play the audio and have students read along.

OVERVIEW OF THE READING

The passage introduces and compares geotourism to mass tourism. It also features an interview with Jonathan Tourtellot, a geotourism advocate and the founding director of the Destination Stewardship Center. As the damage that mass tourism causes to natural locations and local communities becomes more apparent, Tourtellot believes we should adopt a geotourism approach for a more sustainable way of traveling the world. Geotourism involves respecting the geographical diversity of a place and aiming to have a more local experience when traveling. Geotravelers eat locally, stay locally, and join in experiences run by locals so they can experience the culture and history of a place more deeply. Geotourism helps the local community earn a livelihood from tourists without sacrificing the

place where they live. The passage is based on the article *One on One: Jonathan Tourtellot* by Daniel Westergren, which appeared in *National Geographic Traveler*.

Online search terms: geotourism, Destination Stewardship Center, Jonathan Tourtellot

 UNDERSTANDING THE READING
(pages 106–107)

A Understanding Key Terms

Students are asked to choose the three statements that best describe geotourism.

* Have students work individually to complete the activity.
* Check answers as a class. Discuss why the other options are not suitable.

B Understanding Main Ideas

Students are asked to choose the four statements that express Tourtellot's view on tourism.

* Have students work in pairs to complete the activity.
* Check answers as a class. Discuss where students found the answers.

C Understanding Purpose

Students are asked to match a place mentioned in the reading with the reason it was mentioned.

* Have students work individually to complete the activity.
* Check answers as a class. Ask students where they found the answers.

D Critical Thinking: Identifying Arguments

The *Critical Thinking* box explains that writers often make an argument by contrasting pros and cons, or advantages and disadvantages. It provides a list of questions that students can think about when evaluating the strength of an argument. Review the questions before students attempt the exercise.

* Allow students time to refer to the reading and complete the details. Note that the information for this exercise can be found in Paragraphs C, D, G, H, and I.
* Check the answers as a class.

E Critical Thinking: Evaluating Arguments

Students are asked to evaluate the author's argument for geotourism and decide whether it is presented effectively.

- Have students work alone to write notes for questions **1** and **2** before discussing in pairs or in small groups.
- Discuss answers as a class. Ask for volunteers to share their opinions and the reasons for them.

ANSWER KEY

UNDERSTANDING THE READING

A 2, 3, 5 (See Paragraphs D and E.)

B 2 (See Paragraph F.);

3 (See Paragraph G.);

4 (See Paragraph H.);

5 (See Paragraph I.)

(Note that the interview questions provide enough information to identify where each main idea is located.)

C 1. d (See Paragraph E.)

2. b (See Paragraph F.)

3. a (See Paragraph G.)

4. c (See Paragraph I.)

D **Advantages of Geotourism:** local economy / local community; nature and culture / history and culture; geographical diversity / historic places

Disadvantages of Mass Tourism: the local economy; understanding; lose

E Answers will vary. Possible answers:

1. Promoting geotourism may require government-funded advertising. This money could be better used in direct preservation efforts. / Geotourism is still a form of tourism. Tourism changes local places and negatively affects the environment.

2. I agree with the writer's argument. While mass tourism may have financial benefits, the negative impact is too great to ignore. We need to change the way we travel around the world. (Note that this question refers to the views presented in Paragraphs C and D, not to the interview with Jonathan Tourtellot.)

DEVELOPING READING SKILLS
(page 108)

Reading Skill: Analyzing Causes and Effects

The *Reading Skill* box introduces some common words and phrases used to signal a cause-effect relationship. It also explains that writers do not always use these words, and that readers sometimes need to identify this relationship through context.

A Identifying Causes and Effects

Students are asked to find the signal phrase in each item, and identify whether it signals a cause or an effect. Note that there is only one phrase per item.

- Have students work individually to complete the exercise.
- Have them compare their answers in pairs.
- Check answers as a class.

B Analyzing Causes and Effects

Students complete the chart of causes and effects based on Paragraphs C and D of the reading. Note that item 1 in the "Causes" column corresponds to item 1 in the "Effects" column, and so on.

- Have students work in pairs to complete the exercise. Allow them time to look back at the reading if necessary.
- Check answers as a class. Note that students will be asked to identify the signal phrases for each item in the next exercise.

C Analyzing Causes and Effects

Students are asked to identify the words or phrases that were used in the reading to signal the cause-effect relationship. Note that in some cases, there is no signal phrase because the relationship can be understood only through context.

- Have students work in pairs to complete the exercise.
- Check answers as a class. For each item, get volunteers to explain how they arrived at their answer.

DEVELOPING READING SKILLS

A **1.** <u>As</u> ecotourism can bring many benefits, many local and national governments are researching ways to preserve their distinctive natural areas.

2. In Costa Rica, for example, an interest in developing ecotourism **led to** the creation of several national parks and reserves where wildlife is protected.

3. The creation of national parks and reserves requires large numbers of skilled workers. **Consequently**, many people who are out of work may become employed.

4. The government of Costa Rica created a successful international ecotourism marketing campaign. **As a result**, tourism to the country increased dramatically.

B Answers will vary. Possible answers:

1. Cause: Many of the systems that support mass tourism are often owned and run by companies based outside the tourist areas.

2. Cause: Tourists have little or no contact with local people.

3. Effect: Travelers have a broader understanding of the area's history and culture.

4. Effect: The money helps local people earn a living and protects the area.

C **1.** *Much of the money made from this type of tourism does not, <u>therefore</u>, benefit the local economy.*

2. inferred from context (Explanation: …*with mass tourism, visitors do not usually have much contact with the local people. This limits their understanding…*)

3. *<u>As a result</u>, these travelers have a broader…*

4. inferred from context (Explanation: …*the money they spend stays in the local community. This helps local people earn a living…*)

Video

 VIEWING: GALÁPAGOS TOURISM
(pages 109–110)

Overview of the Video

The video explores the effect that tourism has had on the Galápagos Islands in Ecuador, and explains efforts that are being made to reverse some negative impacts. Human activities on and near the islands are causing the natural environment to suffer. Now the government is working together with environmental groups and the local community to make the islands "greener" by being less dependent on nonrenewable resources.

Online search terms: Galápagos Islands, Galápagos renewable energy

BEFORE VIEWING

A Predicting

Students think about the potential effects of tourism on the Galápagos Islands.

• Have students work in pairs to answer the question.

• Discuss answers as a class.

B Learning About the Topic

The paragraph prepares students for the video by giving them background information about the Galápagos Islands and the reasons why they are a hot spot for tourism.

• Have students read the paragraph individually.

• Have them work in pairs to answer the questions.

• Elicit a class discussion. Ask students to add any additional background information they know about the islands or its unique wildlife.

C Vocabulary in Context

This exercise introduces students to some of the key words used in the video. Students use context to deduce the meaning of the words.

• Have students work on the exercise individually.

• Ask them to form pairs to check answers.

• Discuss answers as a class. Elicit example sentences for each word.

BEFORE VIEWING

A   Answers will vary. Possible answer:

The animals don't see humans as a threat. / The area where animals live might become smaller.

B 1. There are thousands of (animal and plant) species, many of which are unique to the islands.

   2. Darwin's study of the animals led to the conclusion that animals adapt to their environments. This observation influenced his famous theory of evolution.

C 1. revenue

   2. contaminant

   3. ruin

   4. wake-up call (Note: This meaning here of *wake-up call* is figurative. The literal meaning of *wake-up call* refers to a phone call that a hotel makes to a hotel guest to wake them up in the morning.)

WHILE VIEWING

A ▶ Understanding Main Ideas

Have students read the items before you play the video.
• Have them complete the task while the video is playing.
• Check answers as a class.

B ▶ Understanding Details

Have students read the items and check any answers they recall from the first viewing before playing the video a second time.
• Play the video again. Have them complete the task while the video is playing.
• Check answers as a class.

WHILE VIEWING

A   1, 3, 4

B   1, 3, 4, 5

AFTER VIEWING

A Reacting to the Video

Students are asked for their opinions on two different arguments related to tourism on the Galápagos Islands.
• Allow students time to read the statements and write notes about their opinions and the reasons for them.
• Have students discuss in pairs or in small groups. Tell them to share the reasons for their opinions.
• Discuss as a class. Separate the class into two groups: those in favor of the first statement and those in favor of the second. Get each group to take turns sharing a reason for their stand.

B Critical Thinking: Synthesizing

Students are asked to apply the ideas of geotourism from Reading 1 or their own ideas to the situation in the Galápagos Islands.
• Allow time for students to go back and review Reading 1, if necessary. Tell them they can also use their own ideas to answer the question.
• Have them brainstorm ideas in pairs or in small groups.
• Discuss the ideas as a class. Ask each group to share one idea that could benefit the islands.

AFTER VIEWING

A   Answers will vary. Possible answers:

I agree with the second statement. As long as efforts are being made, I think tourism is OK. With local cooperation and help from international organizations, I think the situation on the islands is going to improve. And the money from tourism is helping to fund all these efforts.

B   Adopting a geotourism approach may help the Galápagos Islands, as the approach helps preserve the natural environment and support local businesses.

Reading 2

PREPARING TO READ *(page 111)*

A Building Vocabulary

The paragraphs contain ten key vocabulary items that appear in the passage. Students should use contextual clues to deduce the meaning of the words.

- Have students complete the task individually.
- Check answers as a class. Elicit example sentences for each vocabulary item.

B Using Vocabulary

Students should use the new vocabulary items while discussing the question.

- Have students work in pairs to answer the question. Ask them to try to use as many new vocabulary words as possible in their discussion.
- Discuss as a class. Elicit example answers from students.

C Skimming

Students are asked to skim the passage and answer two questions about its content.

- Have students read the question items.
- Allow time for students to skim the passage and write notes for each question.
- Have students form pairs to share their answers. Revisit this exercise after students have completed the reading.

ANSWER KEY

PREPARING TO READ

A

1. objective	**6.** enriching
2. comfort	**7.** official
3. awareness	**8.** landmark
4. renewable	**9.** spiritual
5. vital	**10.** ecological

B Answers will vary. Possible answers:

I went to Canada last summer. My objective was to learn English, but the best part of my trip was meeting so many great people, especially my host family. It was an enriching experience.

C Answers will vary. Suggested answers:

1. The reading passage describes natural locations in Ecuador, Nepal, and Australia.

2. Each place has developed successful ecotourism options that are alternatives to mass tourism.

🎧 1.10 Have students read the passage individually, or play the audio and have students read along.

OVERVIEW OF THE READING

The passage explains three different ways that ecotourism is having a positive impact. First, in Ecuador, locally owned ecolodges provide a way for tourists to experience the country's rich variety of ecosystems while interacting with locals and buying souvenirs directly from the community. Next, three women have created new opportunities for local women in Nepal by forming a women-only trekking guide organization. Not only does their company empower Nepalese women, it also offers female tourists a comfortable, safe, and positive experience while trekking in Nepal. Lastly, Uluru in Australia has long been a popular tourism spot. However, for the indigenous people, the rock is a sacred place and not to be climbed. Now with government support, tourists are prevented from climbing the rock. Instead, they learn about the traditional stories and culture of the Anangu.

Online search terms: Ecuador's ecolodges, 3 Sisters Adventure Trekking, Empowering Women of Nepal, Uluru climbing ban

UNDERSTANDING THE READING *(pages 115–116)*

A Understanding Main Ideas

Students match each section of the reading passage to its main ideas.

- Have students work individually to complete the exercise.
- Check answers as a class.

B Understanding Details

Students match each paragraph or section of the reading passage to a suitable description.

- Have students work individually to complete the exercise.
- Check answers as a class. Discuss where students found the relevant information.

C Inferring Meaning

Students first find and underline the words in the passage. Then they use context to deduce the meaning of the words. Lastly, they note the part of speech and write definitions in their own words.

- Have students work in pairs to locate the words in the passage and deduce their meaning.
- Have students check their answers in pairs.
- Check answers as a class. Get volunteers to share their definitions.

D Analyzing Causes and Effects

Students practice the reading skill introduced earlier in the unit.

- Have students work in pairs to read the sentence and identify the cause and effect before underlining the signal phrase.
- Check answers as a class.

E Critical Thinking: Synthesizing

Students look back at the reading to find examples of geotourism based on Jonathan Tourtellot's description.

- Have students work in pairs. Allow them time to refer to the passage to find examples.
- Check answers as a class. Discuss where students found the relevant information and why it is a form of geotourism.

F Critical Thinking: Evaluating/Justifying

Students pick a destination from the reading and give reasons why it is the best example of geotourism.

- Have students work individually to write their ideas.
- Have them share their opinions in small groups.
- If time permits, discuss as a class. Ask volunteers to share their opinions and the reasons for them.

ANSWER KEY

UNDERSTANDING THE READING

A 1. b (See Paragraph E: …*with two main goals: to give local women opportunities to work in the tourism industry, and to give female trekkers the choice of female guides for greater comfort and security.*)

2. a (See Paragraph B: …*an ecolodge is a type of hotel that helps local economies and protects the environment.*)

3. b (See Paragraph F: *The training program includes classes in English, health, and awareness of ecological issues.*)

4. a (See Paragraph C: *There are ecolodges throughout the country, so visitors can choose to stay in the rain forest, in the mountains, or at an island beach.*)

5. c (See Paragraph I: *While 74 percent of visitors climbed Uluru in 1990, that number dropped to less than 30 percent by 2015.*)

6. c (See Paragraph J: *Instead of taking tourists to the top of the rock, tour guides lead tourists around Uluru on paths that Anangu ancestors walked.*)

B 1. D
2. B
3. C
4. F–G
5. J
6. E
7. H-I

C 1. livelihood (noun): a way of making money to support oneself or one's family
2. ambassador (noun): a representative
3. hot spot (noun): a popular location
4. indigenous (adjective): local, native

D Director of the company, Jascivan Carvalho, says that this kind of travel experience can <u>lead to</u> "a deeper, more enriching experience for travelers, and for locals, whose livelihoods improve."

Answers will vary. Possible answer:

Ecotourism allows visitors to fully experience a place and provides locals with job opportunities at the same time.

E Answers will vary. Possible answers:

Ecolodges in Ecuador: built with renewable materials; some are owned by local people, community can sell local products there; visitors get to know geographical diversity of region by staying at different lodges; visitors meet local people, interact with them, and learn about their culture

Adventure Trekking in Nepal: provides opportunities for local women to work in the male-dominated field of trekking; tourists interact with local guides, visitors learn about culture from guides

Cultural Tours in Australia: respectful of the spiritual significance of the location for local people; indigenous guides are employed; tourists have a deeper cultural exchange and learn about the place instead of just climbing the rock

F Answers will vary. Possible answer:

Place: Uluru

Reason: The government and tour companies made efforts to encourage tourists to enjoy a destination in a way that protects the place. Tourists used to come to climb the rock, but now they are coming to learn about the culture and heritage related to the location, and to show their respect for it.

Writing

OVERVIEW

In this section, students learn how to write a cause-effect essay. The lesson starts by teaching students how to use *if*-clauses for describing a cause and its effect. It then shows students how to expand on a cause-effect paragraph. In the *Writing Task*, students apply these lessons by writing and revising an essay about the positive or negative effects of tourism on a specific location. Students begin with a brainstorming exercise before selecting and organizing their ideas in an outline. Students then draft their essays, revise their drafts, and correct common mistakes related to the use of *if*-clauses.

EXPLORING WRITTEN ENGLISH
(pages 117–119)

A Noticing

Students look at two sentences and decide which part of each sentence is the cause and which is the effect. This exercise is to be done before going over the information in the *Language for Writing* box.

- Explain that these sentences do not have the signal phrases that they learned about in the unit's reading skill.
- Have students complete the task individually.
- Check answers as a class. Point out that *if* introduces the cause regardless of whether it is in the first or second clause of the sentence.

Language for Writing: Using *if …, (then) …*

The *Language for Writing* box introduces how to use an *if*-clause to explain a cause-effect relationship. Explain that the *if*-clause introduces the cause, and the other clause introduces the effect, regardless of the order. Point out that when the *if*-clause comes first in a sentence, it should be followed by a comma.

B Language for Writing

Students practice combining two sentences into one using an *if*-clause.

- Tell students to refer to the information in the *Language for Writing* box as they complete the exercise.
- Have students work individually before comparing answers in pairs.
- Check answers as a class.

C Language for Writing

Students use their own ideas to complete three sentences that describe cause-effect relationships with *if*-clauses.

- Students can use ideas they read about in the unit to help them complete the sentences.
- Have students work individually to complete the exercise.
- Check answers as a class. Elicit example sentences from volunteers.

ANSWER KEY

EXPLORING WRITTEN ENGLISH

A 1. <u>If tourists stay at large international hotels</u>, **they often interact less with locals**.

2. Tourists don't necessarily help the local economy <u>if they only eat at chain restaurants</u>.

LANGUAGE FOR WRITING

B 1. Cause: You buy locally made products.

If you buy locally made products, you support the local economy.

2. Cause: Too many people visit them.

If too many people visit forests and beaches, they might be ruined.

3. Cause: The porters are female.

If the porters are female, female trekkers feel more comfortable and safe.

4. Cause: They stay at an ecolodge.

If tourists stay at an ecolodge, they can learn about local customs.

C Answers will vary. Possible answers:

1. mass tourism continues in the Galápagos

2. they can learn more about the culture and customs

3. they learn the local language and interact with people there

4. You will have a more memorable experience

Writing Skill: Writing a Cause-Effect Essay

The *Writing Skill* box introduces how to write an essay that focuses on effects. Explain that for this kind of cause-effect essay, the thesis statement states that the focus of the essay is on the effects (as opposed to causes). Each body paragraph would then have a topic sentence about one effect, and focus on that. In an essay about causes, the thesis statement and topic sentences would be about causes. Remind students that body paragraphs should also contain details such as examples, statistics, quotations, or reasons to support the topic sentences.

D Analyzing a Cause-Effect Outline

Students are asked to complete an outline for a pro and con essay on the negative effects of vacation rentals. A vacation rental is a house that is rented out short term to visiting tourists. Tell students to use the tips in the *Writing Skill* box if necessary.

- Have students work on the exercise individually.
- Have them check their answers in pairs.
- Discuss the exercise as a class. Can students think of any additional effects that might make the essay stronger?

E Improving a Cause-Effect Paragraph

Students are asked to improve a body paragraph by matching suitable details to the prompt questions.

- Have students work on the exercise individually.
- Have them check their answers in pairs.
- Check answers as a class. Ask students to identify what kind of support (reason, example, etc.) is being added in each case.

F Writing a Cause-Effect Paragraph

Students are asked to use the extra details provided in exercise **E** to rewrite the paragraph. Encourage students to use their own words in their sentences.

- Have students work on the exercise individually.
- Have them form pairs to share their paragraphs.
- Discuss the exercise as a class. Ask for volunteers to share their paragraphs.

WRITING TASK *(page 120)*

A Brainstorming

Read the *Goal* box aloud so students are familiar with the writing task before brainstorming. The aim is for them to choose a location that they know well and list the negative or positive effects of tourism there.

- Get students to first choose a location that they know well, then list the positive and negative effects.
- Allow them time to note their ideas individually first.
- Then have students share and discuss with a partner. Have partners give feedback or any additional ideas.

B Planning

Students complete the outline for their essays. Note that they should focus on either negative OR positive effects, not both. Students should also make notes for supporting details, as well as the introductory and concluding paragraphs.

- Explain that students can use ideas from the unit to support their essays. Encourage them to think about geotourism or ecotourism in these places.
- Allow students time to complete their outlines individually. If necessary, let them go online to get more details for their body paragraphs. Provide assistance as needed.

C First Draft

Have students write a first draft of their essays based on their outline.

- Remind students to use *if*-clauses and signal phrases for cause-effect relationships when needed.
- Allow students time to complete the task individually. Provide assistance as needed. Refrain from error correction at this point.

ANSWER KEY

WRITING TASK

A   Answers will vary. Possible answers:

Topic: Ecuador's ecolodges

Positive Effects: visitors get to learn about the natural environment; support the local community; interact with the local community

Negative Effects: building lodges in natural environments risks harming that environment; possible environmental damage by tourists

B   Answers will vary. Possible answer:

Thesis Statement: While there is some concern about building vacation lodges in places of nature, ecolodges have had many positive effects on small communities in Ecuador.

Effect 1: the building process benefits the local community

Supporting Idea 1 / Details: local people are involved; local labor is used; supports their livelihood

Summary Statement: Ecuador's ecolodges have brought many positive benefits to local communities.

Final Thought: Ecuador's successful ecolodges should be used as a model for other tourism destinations around the world.

REVISING PRACTICE *(page 121)*

The *Revising Practice* box contains an exercise that demonstrates several ways students can improve their first drafts.

- Allow students time to analyze the draft and complete the exercise. Note that this essay is based on the outline used for exercise **D** of the *Exploring Written English* section.
- Check answers as a class. Ask students to explain how each change makes the revised draft stronger.

D Revised Draft

Students should apply the revision techniques used in the *Revising Practice* box to their own drafts, where applicable.

- Explain to students that they will be using the questions as a guide for checking and improving their drafts.
- As a class, review the questions carefully to make sure students understand them.
- Allow students time to revise their essays.

EDITING PRACTICE

The *Editing Practice* box trains students to spot and correct common errors related to *if*-clauses, especially in regard to the use of commas and the correct tense. As a class, go over the information in the box carefully to make sure students understand what to look for.

- Allow students time to complete the exercise individually.
- Check answers as a class by asking students to read out their corrected sentences and explain the errors.

ANSWER KEY

REVISING PRACTICE

1.   c, b, a

2. d. If vacation rentals are empty for days at a <u>time, small</u> grocers and other neighborhood businesses don't have a lot of customers.

   e. Sentence to cross out: Rental companies don't always know everything about the home or apartment owners' backgrounds.

   f. If there are fewer apartments <u>available, rents</u> tend to go up, forcing people with average incomes to move outside of the city.

EDITING PRACTICE

1. If prices are too <u>high, people</u> might stop traveling.

2. If travel <u>journalists write</u> about the importance of protecting destinations, they might educate tourists.

3. If tourists only eat at chain restaurants, they <u>don't</u> learn anything about local food.

4. Tourists show disrespect to the local <u>culture if</u> they climb Uluru.

5. Local communities can benefit if <u>tourism promotes</u> local businesses.

E Final Draft

Have students apply the skills taught in *Editing Practice* to their own revised drafts and check for any other errors.

- Allow students time to edit their drafts.
- Walk around and monitor students as they work. Provide assistance as needed.
- Collect students' work once they have completed it.
- For the next class, show anonymous examples of good essays and common errors.

Ideas for ... EXPANSION

Have students work in groups of three to help review and edit each other's essays further. Ask each student to read another group member's essay and do the following:

- Correct one error in grammar, spelling, etc.
- Give one compliment.
- Give one piece of feedback to help improve the essay.

Allow students time to read each other's essays, take notes, and then discuss their feedback.

 UNIT REVIEW

Students can work in groups on this recap of the unit. For question **1**, encourage students to use the target vocabulary words when appropriate. For questions **2** and **3**, encourage them to check the relevant pages of the unit for answers.

- Allow students time to answer the three questions in groups.
- Ask each group to present its answer for **1**.

INFORMATION DESIGN

6

UNIT OVERVIEW

This unit focuses on the elements that make infographics effective, and why these elements are important. From using accurate and objective information to taking into consideration the cultural background of the audience, effective infographics are more than just something interesting to look at. As visual data becomes more prevalent in journalism and education, students will benefit from knowing how to evaluate whether an infographic contains information that is useful and is presented in a fair manner.

- **READING 1:** Information is increasingly being presented in visual form, and it's important that creators offer a balanced and honest interpretation of the data.

- **VIDEO:** An infographic designer talks about how he aims to create graphics that are informative as well as impressive.

- **READING 2:** Visual symbols are not a universal language; culture and written language play an important part in each country's style of infographics.

Students draw on what they have read and watched to write a persuasive essay about a topic of their choice. The unit prepares them for the writing task by introducing vocabulary for talking about visual data, and by showing how to identify arguments and counterarguments. Students are then taught how to describe visual information, and introduced to the main components of a persuasive essay. Finally, the unit takes students through the steps of brainstorming and planning, and shows them how to revise and edit their essays.

 THINK AND DISCUSS *(page 123)*

The infographic shows the trajectory of some of NASA's satellites as they circumnavigate the Earth. The title and questions help prepare students for the subject matter covered in the unit.

- Have students study the picture, title, and captions.
- Discuss the infographic as a class. Do students think this visual is attractive? Is it easy to understand?
- Discuss the two questions as a class. For question **1**, ask students where they got the answer from. For question **2**, have the class brainstorm a list of different ways in which visual data can be presented.

ANSWER KEY

THINK AND DISCUSS

Answers will vary. Possible answers:

1. The infographic shows the paths of NASA's satellites, which circle around the globe daily collecting information related to land, ocean, atmosphere, solar radiation, etc.

2. In addition to infographics, information can be presented visually in graphs, charts, mind maps, diagrams, etc.

 EXPLORE THE THEME *(pages 124–125)*

The opening spread includes an infographic that explains the many parts of an automobile, and details where each part comes from. It is an example of how information can be presented in a visual format.

- Allow time for students to study the spread and answer the questions individually.
- Check answers as a class. For question **1**, note that the infographic gives three pieces of information about each car part (its name; where it was made; where the headquarters of the supplier is). For question **2**, point out that students should evaluate the infographic and give reasons for their opinions.
- Elicit example sentences from students for each blue word.

Ideas for … EXPANSION

Have students work in pairs or groups to brainstorm ways to improve the infographic in the *Explore the Theme* section. Explain that they are going to make a new infographic. Tell them to use some or all of the information from the infographic, but to make a new visual. Have them present their infographics to the class, explaining why they decided to show the information in that particular way.

Reading 1

30 MINS PREPARING TO READ *(page 126)*

A Building Vocabulary

The sentences in the box contain seven vocabulary items that appear in the reading passage. Students should use contextual clues to identify the part of speech of the vocabulary items, deduce their meaning, and match them to their definitions.

• Have students work individually to complete the exercise.

• Check answers as a class. Elicit example sentences for each vocabulary item.

See Vocabulary Extension 6 in the Student Book for additional practice with mis-.

B Using Vocabulary

Students should use the new vocabulary items while discussing the two questions.

• Have students work in pairs to answer the questions. If necessary, provide prompts to help with their discussion.

• Check answers as a class. Elicit example answers from students.

C Brainstorming

Students are asked to think about the benefits of infographics.

• Ask them to think about the question before forming pairs to discuss it. Encourage them to consider how infographics help them learn or share information.

• Allow pairs time to share and discuss their answers.

• Discuss answers as a class. Elicit ideas from each pair.

D Predicting

Students are asked to skim the first sentence of each paragraph before answering the question.

• Allow students time to skim the passage and predict the topic.

• Revisit this exercise after students have completed the reading.

PREPARING TO READ

A **1.** downside

2. deliberately

3. vision

4. faulty

5. objective (Note: This is an adjective. The noun *objective* refers to a goal or an aim.)

6. neutral

7. misleading (Note: Both the adjective *misleading* (Paragraph E) and the verb *mislead* (Paragraph D) appear in the reading passage.)

B   Answers will vary. Possible answers:

1. One downside is that it's hard to know if the information is reliable.

2. Sometimes people post fake pictures to make themselves famous. Once, I saw a misleading picture of a man who said he'd climbed K2, but the picture turned out to be fake.

C   Answers will vary. Possible answer:

Infographics explain information efficiently, which can be useful for explaining complex concepts in a business meeting or in class. Using infographics in news publications can help engage readers as the information is more interesting to look at.

D   Answers will vary. Correct answer: c

🎧 **2.01**   Have students read the passage individually, or play the audio and have students read along.

OVERVIEW OF THE READING

The passage talks about the growing prevalence of infographics in journalism, and discusses some advantages and disadvantages to presenting information visually. While visuals are a powerful way to present complex data, they also make it easy to misrepresent data and mislead readers. Visual data makes information appear more credible, and people are more likely to believe an infographic than if the same data is presented in writing. Ultimately, infographic designers need to find a balance between visual appeal and the amount of information to present. They also need to ensure that information is presented objectively. This passage is based on the articles *The "Rules" of Data Visualization Get an Update* by Geoff McGhee, and *A Quick Guide to Spotting Graphics That Lie* by Chiqui Esteban.

Online search terms: The "Rules" of Data Visualization Get an Update, A Quick Guide to Spotting Graphics That Lie

UNDERSTANDING THE READING
(pages 130–131)

A Summarizing

Students are asked to complete a summary of the passage by selecting three additional sentences to follow the one provided.

- Have students complete the activity individually.
- Check answers as a class. Discuss where students found the answers.

B Understanding Details

Students are asked to answer questions about details provided from Paragraph C onward.

- Allow students time to look back at the reading. Encourage them to find the details by scanning. For example, they can scan for the name *Cairo* to look for information related to questions **1** and **2**.
- Check answers as a class. Discuss where students found the answers.

C Interpreting Visual Information

Students are asked to match Figures 1–3 to the descriptions.

- Have students work in pairs to complete the activity. If necessary, explain that the *y-axis* refers to the vertical axis for item **a**.
- Check answers as a class. Elicit more details about the descriptions. For example, for item **a**, what is misleading about the figure's y-axis scale?

D Inferring Meaning

Students first find and underline the words in the passage. Then they use context to deduce the meaning of the words. Lastly, they match the sentence parts to complete the definitions.

- Have students work in pairs to locate the words in the passage and deduce their meaning.
- Check answers as a class. Elicit example sentences for each word.

E Critical Thinking: Evaluating Visual Data

The *Critical Thinking* box explains how to evaluate visual data. Tell students to consider the points that they read about in the passage: Is the information presented objectively? Is it misleading? Does the designer or publication have an aim other than a journalistic one? For the exercise, students are given two graphs that present the same data differently.

- Allow students time to study the two graphs.
- Have them work individually to complete the exercise.
- Check answers as a class. Why is each graph better for a particular situation?

F Critical Thinking: Evaluating Infographics

Students are asked to find two infographics from an earlier unit and evaluate them.

• Have students work in pairs. Allow them time to find two infographics and discuss them.

• Discuss as a class. Ask for volunteers to share which infographics they talked about and what their evaluations are. Ask them to make suggestions to improve the one that isn't as effective.

ANSWER KEY

UNDERSTANDING THE READING

A 2, 3, 6

B **1.** Alberto Cairo says visual data is most effective when the information provides "spontaneous insight" / when the information is immediately clear. (See Paragraph C.)

2. Charts make information look more credible or scientific. (See Paragraph D.)

3. when a graph presents faulty logic (Paragraph E); when the scale is inappropriate (Paragraph G); and when a graph is designed to influence a point of view (Paragraph H).

4. Compared to traditional graphs, modern infographics use thousands of data points. (See Paragraph I.)

C **a.** 3 (Explanation: The y-axis (vertical axis) only goes from 40 to 55.)

b. 1 (Explanation: Temperatures are shown to have risen suddenly in the last hundred years.)

c. 3 (Explanation: The difference is actually only about 10 percent, but looks much larger.)

d. 2 (Explanation: The y-axis is performance; the x-axis is time.)

e. 3 (Explanation: The effectiveness of two drugs is compared.)

f. 1 (Explanation: The graph shows various information such as temperatures from different sources, the average temperature, and the time period.)

g. 2 (Explanation: Appearing on the cover has no direct effect on the athletes' performance.)

h. 1 (Explanation: The red and blue lines can be compared against the black line showing the average temperature.)

D **1.** b

2. c

3. d

4. a

E The scale is different—the first graph's y-axis starts from 5.25 percent, while the second one starts from zero percent.

a. 1

b. 2

F Answers will vary. Possible answers:

The infographic in Unit 4, Reading 2 (page 87) gives a very clear and objective description of the supervolcano under Yellowstone National Park.

The infographic in Unit 5's Explore the Theme section could be presented in a more interesting way. Also, the data may be slightly misleading since it may also include people who transited in the city's airport for one night without visiting the city.

 DEVELOPING READING SKILLS
(page 132)

Reading Skill: Identifying Arguments and Counterarguments

The *Reading Skill* box explains that counterarguments are often introduced before the main argument. Presenting the opposite side of an argument actually makes the argument stronger in a persuasive essay. Concession terms like *Although*, *Even though*, and *While* are often used to present a counterargument. In this unit, students learn how to differentiate between arguments and counterarguments.

A Identifying Arguments

Students are asked to refer to the reading and look at sentences that present both arguments and counterarguments.

• Have students work individually to complete the exercise.

• Check answers as a class. Note that students will learn more about counterarguments in the *Exploring Written English* section of Unit 9.

B Identifying Arguments

Students are asked to choose the best paraphrase of each main argument in exercise **A**.

- Have students work individually to complete the exercise.
- Have them compare answers in pairs.
- Check answers as a class. Ask for volunteers to paraphrase the information again in their own words. (For example: 1. Graphs can create a wrong impression about data; 2. There is no cause-effect relationship in this case; 3. Misleading infographics are dishonest journalism; 4. Infographic designers should try to be as objective as possible in presenting data.)

C Identifying Counterarguments

Students match the counterarguments to suitable arguments.

- Have students work individually to complete the exercise.
- Have them form pairs to compare answers.
- Check answers as a class.

ANSWER KEY

DEVELOPING READING SKILLS

A 1. Paragraph E: <u>Even though graphs may look credible,</u> they can be misleading, especially if…

   2. Paragraph F: <u>So, although there may be a correlation between two events,</u> that does not mean that one event has a direct effect on the other;

   3. Paragraph H: <u>While he thinks this may be valid in advertising or PR,</u> it's not a good example of objective journalistic communication.

   4. Paragraph H: <u>Cairo believes that while designers may never be able to approach information in a completely neutral way,</u> they should at least try…

B 1. a
   2. b
   3. b
   4. a

C 1. c
   2. a
   3. b

Video

VIEWING: PAINTING WITH NUMBERS *(pages 133–134)*

Overview of the Video

The video is an excerpt from a *National Geographic Live!* talk by data artist Jer Thorp, who aims to create infographics that impress and inform readers equally. Thorp shows some examples of infographics and explains how and why infographics can engage the general public more effectively than traditional graphs. His complete talk can be found online.

Online search terms: Jer Thorp, Numbers that Paint the Picture

BEFORE VIEWING

A Predicting

Students study the title, photo, and caption and identify what they think the infographic is showing. (Note that this graphic will appear later in the video.)

- Allow students time to study the photo.
- Get students to discuss the two questions in pairs.
- Discuss answers as a class.

B Learning About the Topic

The paragraph prepares students for the video by providing them with some background about the speaker of the video and one of the graphics he speaks about—Florence Nightingale's graphic about causes of death during the Crimean War. Students compare and evaluate their infographics.

- Have students read the paragraph individually. Allow them time to look over Thorp's infographic above again, and to look closely at Nightingale's.
- Have them work in pairs to answer the questions.
- Discuss as a class. Elicit ideas about how the two graphics are similar.

C Vocabulary in Context

This exercise introduces students to some of the key words used in the video. Students use context to deduce the meaning of the words.

- Have students work on the exercise individually.
- Check answers in pairs.
- Discuss as a class. Elicit example sentences for each word.

BEFORE VIEWING

A   Answers will vary. Correct answer:

   1. The colors represent the temperatures of the exoplanets. The sizes represent how big the exoplanets are.

   2. the distance of the exoplanets from their star

B   Both infographics use area/size and color to represent the details.

C   **1.** incidence

   2. plot (Note: The verb *plot* here refers specifically to marking points on graphs, charts, etc.)

   3. angle

   4. strategy

WHILE VIEWING

A ▶ Understanding Main Ideas

Have students read the items before you play the video.

• Have them complete the task while the video is playing.

• Check answers as a class. Are Thorp's ideas about visual data similar to the ideas in Reading 1?

B ▶ Understanding Details

Have students read the questions and write any answers they recall from the first viewing before playing the video a second time.

• Play the video again. Have them complete the task while the video is playing.

• Check answers as a class.

WHILE VIEWING

A   2, 3, 4 (Explanation: Thorp mentions that we visualize data in order to make things simpler to understand and help us learn things we never knew. He also uses the Kepler project as an example of how data can be made more interesting when presented visually.)

B   **1.** suffered from cholera during the cholera epidemic in London

   2. where people are flying to and from

AFTER VIEWING

A Reacting to the Video

Students are asked to read a quote from Thorp's talk and think about its meaning.

• Allow time for students to think about their answer before discussing in pairs.

• Discuss as a class. Ask students to share one example from other units in the textbook of an infographic that has the "ooh-aah" factor.

B Critical Thinking: Applying

Students work in groups to evaluate the infographics that they have seen in earlier units.

• Have students work in small groups. Allow them time to look at earlier units in the book and choose three infographics.

• Ask students to give reasons for their opinions about the "ooh-aah" factor of each infographic.

• Discuss as a class. Which infographic did groups think has the best balance of "ooh" and "aah"?

AFTER VIEWING

A   **1.** when an infographic is attractive or impressive

   2. when they learn something from the infographic

B   Answers will vary. Possible answers:

   Reading 1: easy to understand, but not enough "ohh" as they weren't very interesting to look at / "Just Landed": a good balance of "ohh" and "ahh"; detailed information is not shown but we're able to get a big picture view of world travel by looking at it

Reading 2

30 MINS **PREPARING TO READ** *(page 135)*

A Building Vocabulary

This exercise contains ten vocabulary items that appear in the reading passage. Students should first use a dictionary to check the definition of the words in the box before completing the sentences.
- Have students complete the task individually.
- Check answers as a class. Elicit example sentences for each vocabulary item.

B Using Vocabulary

Students use the new vocabulary items while discussing the questions.
- Have students work in pairs to answer the questions. If necessary, provide prompts to support their discussion.
- Check answers as a class. Elicit example answers from students. For question **1**, ask volunteers to demonstrate gestures and explain their meanings.

C Brainstorming

Students are asked to discuss what they associate the colors red and green with. Note that students will read about how colors have different associations in different cultures.
- Have students work in pairs to discuss the questions.
- Discuss as a class.

D Predicting

Students are asked to predict cultural differences in visual design that they will read about in the passage.
- Allow time for students to read the first paragraph and look at the images.
- Have students discuss in pairs or in small groups. Revisit this exercise after students have completed the reading.

ANSWER KEY

PREPARING TO READ

A 1. Publications, statistics
   2. gestures, emphasize
   3. Nevertheless
   4. context
   5. have to do with
   6. universal, reliance
   7. proposes

B 1. In my country, a common gesture to say "hello" is to wave at someone.
   2. Some topics that have universal appeal include medical topics and environmental topics because these affect us all, regardless of nationality.

C Answers will vary. Possible answer: The color red reminds me of the big sign outside my supermarket, so it makes me hungry. The color green makes me think of nature.

D Answers will vary. Correct answer:
   differences in color, shape, and orientation (left-to-right or right-to-left)

 2.02 Have students read the passage individually, or play the audio and have students read along.

OVERVIEW OF THE READING

The passage explains how culture plays a part in the way visual graphics are presented. In China, for example, red is often used for positive financial values, whereas the same color is usually used for negative values in the United States. In Arabic countries, graphs are often flipped because Arabic is read from right to left. In the reading passage, designers who have worked in countries other than their own discuss what they have learned about how cultural differences affect graphic design preferences. The passage is based on the article *Even Graphics Can Speak with a Foreign Accent* by Chiqui Esteban, which appeared in *National Geographic* magazine.

Online search terms: Even Graphics Can Speak with a Foreign Accent

60 MINS **UNDERSTANDING THE READING**
(pages 139–140)

A Understanding Main Ideas

Students identify three main ideas discussed in the reading passage.
- Have students work individually to complete the activity. Allow them time to refer to the reading, if necessary.
- Check answers as a class.

B Understanding Supporting Ideas

Students answer questions about the details discussed in the reading.

- Have students work in pairs. Encourage them to scan the passage to find the relevant information.
- Check answers as a class. Discuss where students found the answers.

C Critical Thinking: Applying

Students are asked to match three types of publications to suitable characteristics.

- Have students work in pairs to complete the task.
- Allow them time to look back at the passage to find supporting reasons for their answers.
- Check answers as a class.

D Inferring Meaning

Students first find and underline the words in the passage. Then they use context to deduce the meaning of the words. Lastly, they match the sentence parts to complete the definitions.

- Have students work individually to locate the words in the passage and deduce their meaning.
- Have them check answers in pairs.
- Check answers as a class. Elicit example sentences for each vocabulary item.

E Critical Thinking: Synthesizing

Students decide on the most important guidelines for designing graphics.

- Have students work in pairs or in small groups. Note that the order may vary depending on students' opinions about topics, such as the importance of typeface versus overall visual appeal.
- Ask each group member to share their thoughts about what should be first and last on the list. Then have groups discuss what falls in between, and come up with two additional guidelines.
- Discuss as a class. Ask volunteers to share their guidelines with the class.

F Critical Thinking: Applying

Students analyze the visual design of a magazine or newspaper from their country. Have students prepare ahead of time for this task by asking them to bring in a publication from their country.

- Have students work individually to answer the questions. If students are not able to prepare ahead of time, allow them time to go online and find an online publication to use.

- Have students discuss in pairs or small groups. Ask students to show their partners or groups the publication as they evaluate it. Tell them to also talk about how culture may have influenced the design.
- Discuss as a class. Ask for volunteers to share the publication and their analysis with the class.

Ideas for ... EXPANSION

Expand on the discussion in exercise **F**. Have each student show an example page from the publication that they brought in from their country to the class. Ask the other students to offer observations about the visual design. Then have the student presenting respond to classmates' comments and ideas. Are their observations accurate? Why or why not?

ANSWER KEY

UNDERSTANDING THE READING

A 1, 2, 5

B Answers will vary. Possible answers:

1. Not every culture associates the color green with money.
2. Red is used for positive monetary values in China, as opposed to in the west, where red is used for negative values.
3. the challenges of different font preferences and orientation of visuals
4. Visual layouts in China mirrors the Chinese written language. Both are complicated and contain a lot of information in a small amount of space.
5. He learned a lot about seeing things differently from his Portuguese colleagues.

C 1. c (See Paragraph E: *Arabs write and read from right to left.*) (Note: Traditionally, Chinese is also read from right to left, but this is not mentioned in the reading passage.)

2. b (See Paragraph C: *You could see Chinese newspapers where stock market charts use green for negative values and red for positive ones.*)

3. a (Explanation: It is implied in Paragraphs B and C that the color green is associated with money in the United States.)

4. b (See Paragraph G: *His theory is that Chinese visuals are heavily influenced by Chinese writing: complex symbols with many elements compressed in a reduced space.*)

5. a (See Paragraph H: *The result: greater reliance on infographics—charts, statistics, and graphs—in American sports publications.*)

6. c (See Paragraph D: *In typography, Arabs prefer blade-like typefaces…*)

D **1.** a

2. e

3. d

4. c

5. b

E Answers will vary. Possible answer:

1. be based on sound logic

2. have an objective scale

3. be appropriate for your audience

4. be visually interesting

5. use simple typefaces

Additional guidelines:

takes cultural differences into consideration / not overly complex

F Answers will vary. Possible answers:

1. The publication (a newspaper) uses a few main colors such as orange, green, and red to differentiate the sections.

2. The Lifestyle section contains more images, while the Business section contains mainly text and charts.

Writing

OVERVIEW

In this section, students learn how to write a persuasive essay and use visual information to support their argument. The lesson starts by teaching how to describe visual information by introducing phrases for expressing quantities, and then goes on to explain the basic structure of a persuasive essay. In the *Writing Task*, students apply these lessons by writing and revising a persuasive essay on a topic of their choice. Students begin with a brainstorming and research exercise, before selecting the best ideas and organizing them in an outline. Students then draft their essays, improve their drafts, and correct common mistakes related to describing visual data.

 EXPLORING WRITTEN ENGLISH
(pages 141–143)

A Noticing

Students read descriptions of visual data and match them to their likely percentages. This exercise is to be done before going over the information in the *Language for Writing* box.

- Explain to students that they should only focus on the underlined words.
- Have students complete the task individually.
- Check answers as a class. Ask what helped students determine the percentage for each.

Language for Writing: Describing Visual Information

The *Language for Writing* box explains how to describe visual information. For example, students are taught to capitalize the word "Figure" when referring to a specific diagram that they are citing in their writing, as well as the use of commas. Students are also given a list of words and phrases that help them to present numerical data in word form.

B Language for Writing

Students complete sentences about the information in a graph.

- Have students complete the activity individually.
- Have students form pairs to compare answers.
- Check answers as a class.

C Language for Writing

Students write two more sentences about the information in the graph in exercise **B**.

- Have students complete the activity individually. Ask them to write about information that wasn't in exercise **B**, or to present the same information differently.
- Have students form pairs to compare answers.
- Check answers as a class.

Writing Skill: Writing a Persuasive Essay

The *Writing Skill* box introduces how to write a persuasive essay. The writer's main argument should be presented in the thesis statement, and each body paragraph should focus on a supporting reason. The thesis statement states the writer's position on a specific part of the topic. For the body paragraphs, details—including visual data—help make a persuasive argument sound more credible.

D Writing Skill

Students choose the better topic for a persuasive essay out of two choices. Encourage students to refer to the information in the *Writing Skill* box to help them.

- Have students work individually to complete the activity.
- Have students form pairs to compare their answers. Ask them to share their reasons for choosing each topic.
- Check answers as a class. Elicit reasons why one topic is better than the other.

E Writing Skill

Students are asked to identify the best supporting details for a persuasive essay. Note that the topic of eating insects is used for the *Revising Practice* exercise later on.

- Have students work in pairs to complete the activity.
- Check answers as a class. Elicit reasons for the answers.

ANSWER KEY

EXPLORING WRITTEN ENGLISH

A (Note: Students only need to pay attention to the underlined phrase. The figure numbers were created for the exercise.)

  a. 1

  b. 5

  c. 4

  d. 3

  e. 2

LANGUAGE FOR WRITING

B **1.** four times

  2. more than

  3. twice

  4. a third

  5. less than

C   Answers will vary. Possible answers:

  1. Women and men both spend approximately two hours on social media on a typical weekend.

  2. Men spend less than an hour reading during the weekend.

WRITING SKILL

D **1.** a;   **2.** b;   **3.** b

E **1.** b

  2. a, d

  3. a, b, d, e (Explanation: *c* is too general; *f* is not relevant)

WRITING TASK *(page 144)*

A Brainstorming

Read the *Goal* box aloud so students are familiar with the writing task before brainstorming. The aim of the essay is to write a persuasive argument about a topic of choice. The brainstorming task focuses on choosing a topic, as well as listing reasons to support the argument and possible counterarguments. Finally, students are asked to search online for relevant visual data to use in their essays.

- Have students work individually to brainstorm and write notes.
- Have them work in pairs to share ideas and give each other feedback.
- Allow them time to go online to find visual data related to their topic.

B Planning

Students select the best arguments for their position and complete the outline for their essays.

- Allow students to do some additional research online if necessary. If possible, have students print out the infographic they found and include it in their essays. Tell them to write down the source information for each infographic they use.
- Allow students time to complete their outlines individually. Provide assistance as needed.

C First Draft

Have students write a first draft of their essays based on their outline.

- Remind students to include the source(s) of the infographic(s) they used in their essay.
- Allow students time to complete the task individually. Provide assistance as needed. Refrain from error correction at this point.

REVISING PRACTICE *(page 145)*

The *Revising Practice* box contains an exercise that demonstrates several ways students can improve their first drafts.

- Allow students time to analyze the draft and complete the exercise. Note that this essay is based on the same topic as exercise **E** in the *Exploring Written English* section.
- Check answers as a class. Ask students to identify each change and explain how it makes the revised draft stronger (Sentence **a** is a final thought, **b** is a topic sentence, and **c** is a supporting detail that describes the visual data).

D Revised Draft

Students should apply the revision techniques used in the *Revising Practice* box to their own drafts, where applicable.

- Explain to students that they will be using the questions as a guide for checking and improving their drafts.
- As a class, go over the questions carefully to make sure students understand them.
- Allow students time to revise their essays.

EDITING PRACTICE

The *Editing Practice* box trains students to spot and correct common errors related to describing visual data. As a class, go over the information in the box carefully to make sure students understand what to look out for.

- Allow students time to complete the exercise individually.
- Check answers as a class by asking students to read their corrected sentences aloud and explain the errors.

ANSWER KEY

REVISING PRACTICE

> b, c, a

EDITING PRACTICE

1. Much of the animal is wasted: less than half <u>is</u> used for food.
2. A quarter of people <u>spend</u> more than four hours a day online.
3. As <u>Figure</u> 1 illustrates, approximately a third of the animal is wasted.
4. Two-fifths of the students <u>study</u> in the school library.
5. As Figure 3 <u>shows,</u> more than half of the class prefers to use their phones to take notes.

E Final Draft

Have students apply the skills taught in *Editing Practice* to their own revised drafts and check for any other errors.

- Allow students time to edit their drafts.
- Walk around and monitor students as they work. Provide assistance as needed.
- Collect students' work once they have completed it.
- For the next class, show anonymous examples of good essays and common errors.

Ideas for … EXPANSION

Have students work in groups of three to help review and edit each other's essays further. Ask each student to read another student's essay and do the following:

- Correct one error in grammar, spelling, etc.
- Give one compliment.
- Give one piece of feedback to help improve the essay.

Allow students time to read each other's essays, take notes, and then discuss their feedback.

UNIT REVIEW

10 MINS

Students can work in groups on this recap of the unit. For question **1**, encourage students to use the target vocabulary words when appropriate. For questions **2** and **3**, encourage them to check the relevant pages of the unit for answers.

- Allow students time to answer the three questions in groups.
- Ask each group to present its answer for question **1**.

GLOBAL CHALLENGES

ACADEMIC TRACK
Environmental Science

ACADEMIC SKILLS
READING   Understanding appositives
WRITING   Writing an opinion essay
GRAMMAR   Using adjective clauses
CRITICAL THINKING   Inferring attitude

UNIT OVERVIEW

This unit focuses on how human activity is causing climate change at a rapid rate, as well as the efforts of some people to ensure that we have a more sustainable future. Students learn about the devastating effects of climate change and the steps that can be taken to slow these effects down.

- **READING 1:** Actor turned activist Leonardo DiCaprio introduces his new documentary on climate change, *Before the Flood*.

- **VIDEO:** One man's efforts in recording weather data in the snowy mountains of Colorado has helped scientists understand more about global warming.

- **READING 2:** Eight specific steps toward creating a more sustainable planet are outlined and explained.

Students draw upon what they have read and watched to write an opinion essay about how best to create a more sustainable future. The unit prepares them for the writing task by introducing vocabulary for talking about climate change, as well as how to recognize appositives. It also teaches adjective clauses and introduces the components of an opinion essay. Finally, it takes students through the steps of brainstorming and planning, and shows them how to revise and edit their essays.

THINK AND DISCUSS *(page 147)*

The image (a composite photo) shows the Statue of Liberty, an iconic symbol of the United States, submerged halfway in water. The image shows what could happen if all the world's ice were to melt. The title and questions help prepare students for the subject matter covered in the unit.

- Have students study the picture, title, and caption. Elicit the meaning of *sea level* (the level/height of the sea's surface).
- Discuss the photo as a class. What is this picture making a prediction about?
- Discuss the two questions as a class. For question **1**, ask students to think about cities that they know are situated near the sea, and how those places would be affected by a significant rise in sea level. For question **2**, encourage students to consider what they have studied in other units in this book when discussing answers (for example, population rise, overuse of resources for food shipment, etc.).
- Discuss the title of the unit: *Global Challenges*. What kind of challenges do students think the title refers to? Elicit ideas. (The challenges covered in this unit are mainly to do with the environment and natural resources.)

ANSWER KEY

THINK AND DISCUSS

Answers will vary. Possible answers:

1. Rising sea levels may flood towns and cities built at or close to sea level. Many homes and habitats may be lost.

2. Due to rising temperatures from the effects of climate change, Arctic sea ice is melting, which is contributing to rising sea levels.

EXPLORE THE THEME *(pages 148–149)*

The opening spread contains a map of GDP levels worldwide. Activities that drive economic growth usually consume natural resources. As more countries strive for greater economic growth, it may lead to an increased consumption of our natural resources.

- Allow time for students to study the spread and answer the questions individually.
- Check answers as a class. As the class discuss, revisit the *Think and Discuss* questions about rising sea levels. Is there a connection between GDP growth and rising sea levels?
- Elicit sample sentences from students for each blue word.

Reading 1

30 MINS PREPARING TO READ *(page 150)*

A Building Vocabulary

The sentences in the box are related to the topic of climate change. Students should use contextual clues to deduce the meaning of the words.

- Have students work individually to complete the exercise.
- Check answers as a class. Elicit example sentences for each vocabulary item.

B Using Vocabulary

Students should use the new vocabulary items while discussing the two questions.

- Have students work in pairs to answer the questions. If necessary, provide some prompts to help with their discussion.
- Check answers as a class. Elicit example answers from students.

C Brainstorming

Before reading about climate change, students are asked to think about environmental issues the world faces today and how we can deal with them.

- Ask students to think about the questions individually before discussing in pairs.
- Allow pairs time to share their answers.
- Discuss answers as a class. Elicit opinions and ideas from each pair.

D Predicting

Students are asked to predict topics they will read about by skimming the first part of the reading.

- Allow students time to read the paragraph and questions. Point out that they only need to read the questions, not the answers.
- Have students form pairs to discuss their answers. Revisit this exercise after students have completed the reading.

PREPARING TO READ

A 1. vanish

2. crucial

3. practical

4. generate

5. exceptional

6. focus on

7. shrink

B Answers will vary. Possible answers:

1. One crucial problem in my hometown is that the population is shrinking. Because so many young people are moving to urban areas, many small towns in the countryside are starting to vanish.

2. My country needs to make small towns more appealing for people to live in. One practical solution is to generate job opportunities by bringing more businesses to the countryside.

C Answers will vary. Possible answers:

1. I think the most important environmental issue we face today is rising sea levels.

2. More stories, news reports, and videos about the problem may help educate people. Also, celebrities can help persuade people to take action.

D Answers will vary. Correct answer: DiCaprio talks about his efforts to raise awareness of climate change—making a film to educate people. He also shares his thoughts on why people should take the problem seriously and what they can do about it.

🎧 **2.03** Have students read the passage individually, or play the audio and have students read along.

OVERVIEW OF THE READING

The passage is an excerpt from an interview with actor and environmental activist Leonardo DiCaprio. DiCaprio introduces his new movie, *Before the Flood*, which took him on a journey around the world to learn about climate change. DiCaprio, who speaks to scientists and world leaders in the film, shares what he feels needs to be done to tackle this problem head on: he says governments must get involved. In addition to the interview, the passage also contains information about climate change and the effects it is having on our planet.

This section is adapted from the article *Seven Things to Know About Climate Change*, which appeared in *National Geographic*. Clips of DiCaprio's documentary can be viewed online on various video platforms such as YouTube.

Online search terms: Before the Flood, Seven Things to Know About Climate Change

 UNDERSTANDING THE READING (pages 154–155)

A Understanding Main Ideas

Students are asked to choose the answer that best summarizes the interview with DiCaprio.

- Have students work individually to complete the activity.
- Check answers as a class. Discuss where students found the answers.

B Understanding Main Ideas

Students are asked to complete the sentences about the main ideas of the section *Seven Facts about Climate Change*.

- Have students work in pairs to complete the activity.
- Check answers as a class. Discuss where students found the answers.

C Understanding Details

Students are asked to identify each piece of information as true, false, or not given. The statements all relate to the section *Seven Facts about Climate Change*.

- Have students work individually to complete the activity.
- Check answers as a class. Discuss where students found the answers.

D Interpreting Visual Information

This exercise requires students to look at the information in the five graphs in the reading passage.

- Have students work individually or in pairs to complete the activity. Point out that two descriptions are extra.
- Discuss answers as a class. Which graph is the easiest to understand? Why?

E Critical Thinking: Inferring Attitude

The *Critical Thinking* box explains how to infer an author or speaker's attitude by paying attention to adjectives and modals used. For this exercise, students should refer to Paragraphs D–F and look for expressions that DiCaprio uses.

- Allow students time to reread Paragraphs D–F.

- Discuss the paragraphs as a class. Note that even though DiCaprio mentions about government leadership, the second half of Paragraph F shows that while climate is a very pressing issue now, there is still time for people to do something about it.

F Critical Thinking: Evaluating

Students are next asked to think about their own opinions about the topic in the reading passage.
- Have students work alone to write notes before discussing their views in pairs or small groups.
- Discuss answers as a class. Ask for volunteers to share their opinions and the reasons for them.

ANSWER KEY

UNDERSTANDING THE READING

A 1. b (See Paragraph C: *"We wanted to make a film that gave people a sense of urgency, [and] that made them understand what particular things are going to solve the problem."*)

2. a (See Paragraph B: *DiCaprio became a climate activist after a 1998 meeting with former U.S. Vice President Al Gore, an early advocate for climate change education.*)

3. c (See Paragraph D: *For the film we interviewed inspiring figures, from Pope Francis to President Obama, who both have the ability to galvanize millions of people…*)

B (See *Seven Facts about Climate Change* section.)

1. half-century

2. human, natural

3. scientists, carbon (dioxide)

4. speeding up / intensifying

5. weather, often / frequently

6. vanishing

7. cheaper / less expensive

C 1. T (See Paragraph G: *…the heat in 2016 broke the historic record set in 2015, which broke the one from 2014.*)

2. F (See Paragraph H: *Carbon dioxide warms the planet, and we've increased the amount in the air by nearly half, mostly since the 1960s.*)

3. NG

4. T (See Paragraph J: *Together, these factors contribute to rising sea levels, which could rise by three feet by 2100—or maybe more.*)

5. NG

6. T (See Paragraph L: *A 2016 study showed that of 976 species surveyed, 47 percent had vanished from areas on the warm edge of their range.*)

7. F (See Paragraph M: *By 2040, … solar power prices may decrease by 500 percent.*)

D a. 3

b. 5

c. (extra)

d. 2

e. 4

f. (extra)

g. 1

E b (Paragraph E: *There is no issue this important— because the future of the planet is at stake.* Paragraph F: *We can still prevent these crises from becoming a widespread challenge in the future of our country.*)

F Answers will vary. Possible answer:

I agree with DiCaprio because extreme weather events are becoming increasingly common. I've experienced bad typhoons, too. I think we need to do more to protect the future of our planet.

 DEVELOPING READING SKILLS *(page 156)*

Reading Skill: Understanding Appositives

The *Reading Skill* box gives information about *appositives*—words or phrases that describe nouns in more detail. Made up of nouns or noun clauses, appositives are usually set off by punctuation marks (commas, parentheses, dashes, colons). Appositives can be placed before or after the noun they describe.

A Understanding Appositives

Students are asked to look at sentences from the reading passage and identify the appositives and the nouns they describe.
- Have students work individually to complete the exercise. Do the first question as an example, if necessary.
- Have students form pairs to compare answers.
- Check answers as a class.

B Understanding Appositives

Students complete the sentences with the correct appositives.
- Have students work individually to complete the exercise.
- Have them form pairs to compare their answers.
- Check answers as a class.

C Applying

Students are asked to find two sentences with appositives in the *Explore the Theme* section.
- Have students work in pairs to complete the exercise.
- Check answers as a class.

ANSWER KEY

DEVELOPING READING SKILLS

A 1. <u>Oscar-winning actor</u> **Leonardo DiCaprio** likes to say that he makes his living in made-up worlds.

2. DiCaprio became a climate activist after a 1998 meeting with <u>former U.S. Vice President</u> **Al Gore**, …

3. For the film we interviewed inspiring figures … like **Sunita Narain**, <u>a tremendous voice in India</u> who's calling for her country to be part of a global solution.

4. Events such as **El Niño**—<u>a climate cycle in the Pacific Ocean</u>—also affect global temperatures.

B 1. b

2. a

3. d

4. c

C 1. …*Gross Domestic Product (GDP)*—<u>*the amount of goods, services produced in one year*</u>…

2. …*consumption,* <u>*the using up of resources*</u>.

Video

🕐 **VIEWING: THE SNOW GUARDIAN**
(pages 157–158)

Overview of the Video

The video features a man named billy barr (Note that he spells his first and last name with a lowercase "b"). barr lives on his own in a cabin in the snowy mountains of Colorado. While at first glance he may seem to have a quiet life, he is actually contributing in a very important way to science. Every day for the last 40 years, barr has measured the levels of snow in his area and carefully recorded this information. His data has allowed scientists to analyze the specific effects of climate change over this period of time in his part of Colorado. According to barr's observations, there have been changes in the amount of snowfall as well as how quickly snow melts.

Online search terms: Gothic Colorado, billy barr, Rocky Mountain Biological Laboratory

BEFORE VIEWING

A Predicting

Students are asked to predict the topic of the video.
- Have students study the title, photo, and caption and predict what they may see in the video.
- Discuss as a class.

B Learning About the Topic

The paragraph prepares students for the video by providing them background information about the area that billy barr lives in. Students then answer questions about the information in the paragraph.
- Have students read the paragraph individually.
- Have them work in pairs to answer the questions.
- Have a class discussion. Ask students why they think billy barr chooses to live in a remote place.

C Vocabulary in Context

This exercise introduces students to some of the key words used in the video. Students use context to deduce the meaning of the words.
- Have students work on the exercise individually.
- Have them form pairs to check answers.
- Discuss as a class. Elicit example sentences for each word.

BEFORE VIEWING

A   Answers will vary. Correct answer:

The video is about a man who lives in a remote mountain area and keeps a detailed record of yearly snowfall, and the weather trends he has observed.

B **1.** Gothic was a silver-mining town, and after all the silver was gone, people left.

     2. A research facility was opened in the town in 1928, which brought people back.

     3. Answers will vary. Possible answer: Gothic is a suitable place for research on climate change and local wildlife because it is close to nature and has experienced little impact from human activity over the last hundred years.

C **1.** curiosity

     2. meticulous

     3. reverse

WHILE VIEWING

A ▶ Understanding Main Ideas

Have students read the items before you play the video.
- Have them complete the task while the video is playing.
- Check answers as a class. For question **2**, ask students how barr's attitude toward climate change compares with DiCaprio's in Reading 1. (DiCaprio is more optimistic than barr is about the situation.)

B ▶ Understanding Details

Have students read each item and write any answers they recall from the first viewing before playing the video a second time.
- Play the video again. Have students complete the task while the video is playing.
- Check answers as a class.

WHILE VIEWING

A **1.** a

     2. c

B **1.** snow pack

     2. bare

     3. 4–5, 36

     4. dust

AFTER VIEWING

A Reacting to the Video

Students are asked to imagine themselves living and working in the town of Gothic.
- Allow time for students to think about their responses to the questions before discussing in pairs.
- Discuss as a class. Ask students to consider various situations. For example, would they want to do what billy barr does? Or would they simply like to live in Gothic, or some place similar, and do a different kind of research? What kind of research would they want to do?

B Critical Thinking: Evaluating

Students are asked to think about the possible limitations of billy barr's data and whether it can be considered as a reliable indictor of climate change.
- Have students work in pairs to discuss their thoughts about the questions.
- Have a class discussion. Ask for volunteers to share their views and the reasons for them.

AFTER VIEWING

A   Answers will vary. Possible answers:

Yes, I think working and living close to nature would be quite relaxing and stress-free compared to working in a city. / No, I wouldn't want to live there. I think that type of lifestyle is a little too extreme for me. It's also inconvenient to go anywhere. Plus, I don't like the cold!

B   Answers will vary. Possible answers: The data is only for one small area. And since he is the only one recording the data, there is a chance that it could be inaccurate. / Scientists have probably checked his data before deciding whether it was useful for studying climate change.

Reading 2

⏱ 30 MINS PREPARING TO READ *(page 159)*

A Building Vocabulary

The sentences in the box contain ten key vocabulary items that appear in the reading passage. Students should use contextual clues to deduce the meaning of the words.

- Have students complete the task individually.
- Check answers as a class. Elicit example sentences for each vocabulary item.

See Vocabulary Extension 7 in the Student Book for additional practice with expressions with cut.

B Using Vocabulary

Students should use the new vocabulary items while discussing the questions.

- Have students work in pairs to answer the questions. If necessary, provide prompts to support their discussion.
- Check answers as a class. Elicit example answers from students.

C Predicting

Students are asked to think about some possible ways of creating a sustainable future that are discussed in the reading passage. Note that they are NOT instructed to skim the reading before discussing.

- Ask them to work in pairs to brainstorm ideas about sustainable solutions offered in each section.
- Discuss as a class. Revisit this exercise after students have completed the reading.

ANSWER KEY

PREPARING TO READ

A **1.** control
  2. releases
  3. change
  4. use it up completely
  5. use it up
  6. an important
  7. a decrease
  8. use less of it
  9. not a lot
  10. put money into

B Answers will vary. Possible answers:

My electronic devices and air conditioner consume a lot of electricity because I often leave them plugged in or turned on. I need to cut down on my energy consumption by turning off the devices when they are not in use.

C Answers will vary. Steps listed in the passage:

create sustainable communities; reduce the effects of meat production; use renewable energy; invest money in businesses with good environmental practices; use LED light bulbs; regulate logging and create certified forests; employ more people in the renewable energy industry; lower carbon emissions

---

 2.04 Have students read the passage individually, or play the audio and have students read along.

OVERVIEW OF THE READING

The passage explains eight steps that can help people and countries move toward more sustainable ways of living, which will hopefully reverse or slow down some of the devastating effects of climate change. The passage is an excerpt from *Nine Ways to Make a Difference*, which appeared in *National Geographic EarthPulse State of the Earth 2010*.

Online search terms: sustainable communities, certified forests, socially responsible investing, National Geographic EarthPulse State of the Earth 2010

⏱ 60 MINS UNDERSTANDING THE READING *(pages 163–164)*

A Understanding Main Ideas

Students complete a list of the eight steps to sustainability.

- Explain that the exercise is like a note-taking list, so each statement is a fragment.
- Do the first item as an example for the whole class. *(motivating people to…)*
- Have students work individually to complete the activity.
- Check answers as a class.

B Understanding Problems and Solutions

Students search the sections for supporting details in the form of examples. Note that there is more than one answer in some cases as multiple examples are given.

- Have students work in pairs.
- Allow them time to look at the reading and find examples.
- Check answers as a class. Discuss where students found the relevant information.

C Interpreting Visual Information

Students use the infographic in the reading passage to answer the questions.

- Allow students time to work individually.
- Check answers as a class. Discuss where in the infographic students found the relevant information.

D Inferring Meaning

Students first find and underline the words in the passage. Then they use context to deduce the meaning of the words. Lastly, they write definitions in their own words.

- Have students work in pairs to locate the words in the passage and deduce their meaning.
- Check answers as a class. Tell students that the definitions can be worded differently as long as they express the main meaning of the word.

E Understanding Appositives

Students practice the reading skill introduced earlier in this unit.

- Have students work in pairs to look back at the reading and find examples of appositives.
- Check answers as a class. For each paragraph, have a volunteer read the sentence that contains the noun and its appositive. Ask students what kind of information the appositives add.

F Critical Thinking: Evaluating

Students evaluate the steps mentioned in the reading and share their opinion on the ones they think are most crucial.

- Have students work in groups of three or four.
- Ask them to share which steps they think are the most important, and why.
- If time permits, discuss as a class.

Ideas for … EXPANSION

Have students work in groups. Which of the eight steps can people do on a personal level, and which ones require the cooperation of governments and businesses? For those actions that can be done on a personal level, ask students about the kinds of changes people would need to make to their lifestyles.

ANSWER KEY

UNDERSTANDING THE READING

A
1. motivating
2. making
3. using
4. investing
5. using
6. regulating
7. increasing
8. reducing

B Answers will vary. Possible answers:

1. a community in Senegal uses solar ovens that don't require wood for cooking / public transportation reduces traffic congestion and improves air quality
2. animal waste causes water pollution / risk of dangerous diseases spreading in cities
3. cutting down on landfill waste / creating alternative energy
4. causes water pollution / destroys animal habitats
5. renewable energy industry / wind industry / solar power industry
6. Brazil / India / Nigeria

C
1. a
2. 3
3. China, United States
4. United States
5. China

D Answers will vary. Possible answers:

1. tax break: something the government does that reduces the amount of taxes people or businesses need to pay
2. harvesting: using / gathering / collecting
3. market share: the percentage sales that a business has out of the total sales of a product
4. jointly: together / in collaboration with

E Paragraph F: One method is via the use of **photovoltaic cells (PVs)**, cells that convert solar energy to electricity.

Paragraph I: **Logging**—the cutting down of trees—has several negative effects on the environment.

F Answers will vary. Possible answers:

Cleaner Power; Lower Emissions; Safer Production

I think lowering carbon emissions would help a lot as carbon emissions are one of the major causes of global warming.

Writing

OVERVIEW

In this section, students learn how to write an opinion essay. The lesson starts by teaching restrictive and nonrestrictive adjective clauses, and then introduces the structure of an opinion essay. In the *Writing Task*, students apply these lessons by writing and revising an opinion essay about one way we can achieve environmental sustainability. Students begin with a brainstorming exercise before selecting the best ideas and organizing them in an outline. Students then draft their essays, improve their drafts, and correct common mistakes related to the use of adjective clauses.

EXPLORING WRITTEN ENGLISH
(pages 165–167)

A Noticing

Students decide which sentence contains information that can be left out without affecting its meaning. This exercise is to be done before going over the information in the *Language for Writing* box.

- Have students complete the task individually before discussing in pairs.
- Check answers as a class. Elicit or explain why the information is essential or nonessential (extra) in each sentence (e.g., In sentence 1, if the underlined part is removed, we don't know what kind of leaders the sentence is referring to. The information is incomplete.)

Language for Writing: Using Adjective Clauses

The *Language for Writing* box introduces restrictive and nonrestrictive adjective clauses, also known as relative clauses. Remind students that they learned about appositives earlier in the unit. Like appositives, adjective clauses also help describe or explain a noun better. Adjective clauses give either essential information (restrictive clauses) or nonessential (nonrestrictive clauses). Restrictive clauses give specific information that helps readers understand the noun. Nonrestrictive clauses add information that is not important in understanding the meaning of the noun, and can be removed without changing the meaning of the sentence. Go over each type of adjective clause and explain how the information is essential or extra. Also highlight how commas are used differently.

B Using Restrictive Adjective Clauses

Students practice writing restrictive adjective clauses.
- Quickly review what a restrictive adjective clause is. Go over the example given in the student book as a class.
- Have students complete the activity individually.
- Have students form pairs to compare answers.
- Check answers as a class.

C Using Nonrestrictive Adjective Clauses

Students practice writing nonrestrictive adjective clauses.
- Explain that this time students have to combine the sentences to add nonessential information.
- Check answers as a class. Check that students have used commas in the correct places.

ANSWER KEY

EXPLORING WRITTEN ENGLISH

A 2 (Explanation: The underlined clause is non-essential because it can be removed without affecting the main focus of the sentence.)

LANGUAGE FOR WRITING

B 1. Farms that are close to the city centers increase the risk of dangerous diseases—such as avian flu—spreading.

2. The Thai government placed a high tax on poultry farms that were within 100 kilometers of Bangkok.

3. Sun and wind power are two energy sources that are renewable.

C 1. Beef production, which requires a lot of water, contributes to climate change.

2. The city of Curitiba, which has an efficient bus system, has very little traffic congestion.

3. Leonardo DiCaprio, who is a UN Messenger of Peace, has produced a documentary on climate change.

Writing Skill: Writing an Opinion Essay

The *Writing Skill* box introduces how to write an opinion essay. Explain that for an opinion essay, it is OK if the thesis statement contains a first-person reference because they are sharing their personal opinion. Point out that in most other essay types, the thesis statement usually doesn't include "I" or "my." Also explain that the body paragraphs should each state a reason for the opinion expressed in the thesis statement, as well as supporting details to explain the reasons.

D Analyzing

Students are asked to read a sample outline for an opinion essay and answer questions about it.

- Allow students time to look at the questions before reading the outline.
- Have students work on the exercise individually.
- Have them form pairs to check their answers.
- Discuss as a class. Elicit the answer to each question, going over how the writer is able to express and support the opinion in the outline. Do students think this is going to be a well-supported essay? Tell students that they can use this outline as a reference for their own outlines in the *Writing Task*. (Note that the *Revising Practice* provides an example of a complete essay based on this outline.)

ANSWER KEY

WRITING SKILL

D 1. reducing the problem of climate change (See Thesis Statement.)

2. The writer says that vegetarianism saves resources and slows climate change. (See Thesis Statement.)

3. Vegetarianism saves water and cuts down on carbon emissions. (See Topic Sentences.)

4. First reason: statistics about meat production versus plant production

Second reason: an explanation of how meat production leads to a lot more greenhouse gas emissions

---

WRITING TASK *(page 168)*

A Brainstorming

Read the *Goal* box aloud so students are familiar with the writing task before brainstorming. The aim is to think of different ways a government, a business, or an individual can help create a sustainable future.

- Explain that students should use a chart for their brainstorming. Tell students that they can look back at the unit to get ideas.
- Allow them time to note their ideas individually first.
- Then have students share and discuss their ideas with a partner. Get partners to give additional ideas or offer feedback.

B Planning

Students choose one idea from their brainstorming notes and complete the outline for their essays.

- Explain that students can use information from the reading passages and video to support their opinions. If there is time, allow students to do some additional online research.
- Allow students time to complete their outlines individually. Provide assistance as needed.

C First Draft

Have students write a first draft of their essays based on their outline.

- Remind students to use adjective clauses where suitable.
- Allow students time to complete the task individually. Provide assistance as needed. Refrain from error correction at this point.

WRITING TASK

A Answers will vary. Possible answers:

Individuals: go vegetarian, use LED lightbulbs, invest in socially responsible businesses

Businesses: use renewable energy sources, increase "green" jobs

Governments: set goals to lower carbon emissions, give tax breaks to "green" businesses, reward sustainable communities

B Answers will vary. Possible answer:

Hook/Background Information: people are using more of Earth's resources than nature can replenish, e.g. fresh water

Thesis Statement: In my opinion, becoming a vegetarian is the best way to preserve our resources and slow down global warming because it saves water and cuts down on carbon emissions.

Topic Sentence 1: One reason that vegetarianism is a good way to reduce our use of resources is that it saves large amounts of water.

Details: 1kg of beef = 16,000L; 1kg of corn = 833L

Summary Statement: Not eating meat is a good way to ensure a sustainable future because it uses less water, and it also reduces greenhouse gas emissions.

Final Thought: becoming a vegetarian keeps both the planet and people healthy

REVISING PRACTICE *(page 169)*

The *Revising Practice* box contains an exercise that demonstrates several ways students can improve their first drafts.

- Allow students time to analyze the draft and complete the exercise. Note that this essay is based on the outline used in exercise **D** on page 167.
- Check answers as a class. Ask students to identify each change and explain how it makes the revised draft stronger.

D Revised Draft

Students should apply the revision techniques used in the *Revising Practice* box to their own drafts, where applicable.

- Explain to students that they will be using the questions as a guide for checking and improving their drafts.
- As a class, go over the questions carefully to make sure students understand them.
- Allow students time to revise their essays.

EDITING PRACTICE

The *Editing Practice* box trains students to spot and correct common errors related to adjective clauses, especially the use of commas and relative pronouns. As a class, go over the information in the box carefully to make sure students understand what to look out for.

- Allow students time to complete the exercise individually.
- Check answers as a class by asking students to read their corrected sentences aloud and explain the errors.

REVISING PRACTICE

1. a. Paragraph B
   b. Paragraph D
   c. Paragraph C
2. d. second blank in Paragraph A
   e. first blank in Paragraph A
   f. Sentence to cross out: Producing biofuels from corn and other plants also uses large amounts of water.

EDITING PRACTICE

1. <u>Vegetarianism,</u> which means not eating meat, is one way to reduce greenhouse gas emissions.
2. CFLs, <u>which</u> are popular in countries like Japan, use 75 percent less energy than traditional lightbulbs.
3. Logging <u>that</u> is done without regulation causes many types of environmental harm.
4. Costa Rica, which already generates 80 percent of its energy through renewable <u>sources,</u> has promised to have zero net carbon emissions by 2030.
5. DiCaprio, <u>who</u> is the founder of the Leonardo DiCaprio Foundation, is working to make people aware of the effects of climate change.
6. DiCaprio made a <u>film that</u> gave people a sense of urgency.

E Final Draft

Have students apply the skills taught in *Editing Practice* to their own revised drafts and check for any other errors.

- Allow students time to edit their drafts.
- Walk around and monitor students as they work. Provide assistance as needed.
- Collect students' work once they have completed it.
- For the next class, show anonymous examples of good essays and common errors.

Ideas for … EXPANSION

Have students work in groups of three to help review and edit each other's essays further. Ask each student to read another student's essay and do the following:

- Correct one error in grammar, spelling, etc.
- Give one compliment.
- Give one piece of feedback to help improve the essay.

Allow students time to read each other's essays, take notes, and then discuss their feedback.

 **UNIT REVIEW**

Students can work in groups on this recap of the unit. For question **1**, encourage students to use the target vocabulary words when appropriate. For questions **2** and **3**, encourage them to check the relevant pages of the unit for answers.

- Allow students time to answer the questions in groups.
- Ask each group to present its answer for question **1**.

MEDICAL INNOVATIONS

ACADEMIC TRACK

Health / Medicine

ACADEMIC SKILLS

READING	Understanding passive sentences
WRITING	Evaluating information online
GRAMMAR	Introduction to quoting and citing sources
CRITICAL THINKING	Inferring purpose

UNIT OVERVIEW

This unit focuses on medical innovators and innovations in both ancient and modern times. From reading about a 12th-century pioneer and his definitive medical text, to exploring how modern-day medical practitioners are using technology to improve healthcare, students learn about different people who have contributed to the medical field. The continual advancements in medical technology are allowing people to live healthier and longer lives today.

- **READING 1:** The knowledge and inventions of 12th-century medical pioneer Al-Zahrawi are still influencing how surgeons operate on patients today.

- **VIDEO:** An engineer uses cell phone technology to help diagnose and monitor global epidemics like malaria.

- **READING 2:** Some exciting breakthroughs are happening in the fields of regenerative medicine and nanotechnology.

Students draw on what they have read and watched to write a research-based essay about an innovation in medicine, science, or technology. The unit prepares them for the writing task by introducing vocabulary for talking about innovations, as well as how to identify and understand the passive voice. Students are then taught how to evaluate online information during the research process, and how to cite sources when using direct quotations. Finally, the unit takes students through the steps of brainstorming and planning, and shows them how to revise and edit their essays.

THINK AND DISCUSS (page 171)

The photo shows a picture of a drone delivering medical supplies to a clinic in Virginia, U.S.A. Drones can help deliver medical supplies to remote or hard-to-access places, and may be a way to provide medical care for people in those areas. The title and questions help prepare students for the subject matter covered in the unit.

- Have students study the picture, title, and caption. Elicit the meaning of *innovation* as well as other forms and their meanings (*innovate, innovator*).
- Discuss the photo as a class. What does the picture show? Who might benefit from this technology?
- Discuss the two questions as a class. For question **1**, get students to think about recent medical treatments that are unlikely to have been around 100 years ago. For question **2**, ask students to make predictions based on what they hope will be improved in medicine and medical care. Do they have ideas about how these improvements may happen?

ANSWER KEY

THINK AND DISCUSS

Answers will vary. Possible answers:

1. Hospitals have become more sterile. / Pain treatment has become more effective. / Vaccines have eradicated some diseases.

2. Medical care will become cheaper and more universally accessible. / Cancer will be cured. / The common cold will be cured. / Technology will help prevent disease before it happens.

EXPLORE THE THEME *(pages 172–173)*

The opening spread shows a timeline of some important medical innovations from 400 B.C. to the present.

- Allow time for students to study the spread and answer the questions individually.
- Check answers as a class. For question **1**, point out that students should give reasons for their opinions. For question **2**, have the class brainstorm ideas. Write the innovations in a mind map on the board for students to use in discussions and exercises in the unit. Note that students will be asked again to brainstorm a list of innovations in the *Writing Task*.
- Elicit example sentences from students for each of the blue words.

ANSWER KEY

EXPLORE THE THEME

A   Answers will vary. Possible answers:

1. I think Louis Pasteur's discovery about germs was the most important because it changed how we live every day, how medicine is practiced, and how hospitals are run. Also, there is still so much to learn about bacteria, so microbiology is a very important field of medical research today.

2. Diabetes is a major problem in the world today. These days wearable technology that measure a person's blood sugar levels is available. It uses Bluetooth to upload information so users can check their levels on their smartphone or other devices.

B   method; manage to; pioneer (Note that *manage* has several meanings: here it means *to be able to (do something),* but the verb *manage* can also mean *to be in charge of something).*

Reading 1

PREPARING TO READ *(page 174)*

A **Building Vocabulary**

The sentences in the box contain seven vocabulary items that appear in the reading passage. Students should use contextual clues to deduce the meaning of the words.

- Have students work individually to complete the exercise.
- Check answers as a class. Elicit example sentences for each vocabulary item.

B **Using Vocabulary**

Students should use the new vocabulary items while discussing the questions.

- Have students work in pairs to answer the questions. If necessary, provide some prompts to help with their discussion.
- Discuss as a class. Elicit example answers from students.

C **Brainstorming**

Students are asked to think about the ways medical knowledge has probably been passed down over centuries.

- Ask them to think about the question individually before discussing in pairs.
- Allow pairs time to share and discuss their answers.
- Discuss answers as a class. Ask each pair for their opinions and ideas.

D **Predicting**

Students are asked to predict the topic of the passage by looking at the title and photos.

- Allow students time to look at the title and pictures.
- Have students form pairs to discuss their ideas. Revisit this exercise after students have completed the reading.

PREPARING TO READ

A **1.** existing

    2. concept

    3. general

    4. spread

    5. compile

    6. civilization

    7. manual (Note: the adjective *manual* has a different meaning; it refers to something being done by hand.)

B Answers will vary. Possible answers:

    1. I never read the manual. I always just turn the device on and start playing with it because usually I can figure out how it works this way. Sometimes I also check online for user videos.

    2. Taking notes in an organized fashion is one method I use to learn new concepts. I use visuals such as a mind map to organize my ideas. Before a test, I rewrite my notes in different ways in order to remember them better.

C Answers will vary. Possible answers:

    Medical practitioners probably passed on knowledge by teaching each generation through apprenticeships, and by maintaining an oral history. When written language became more common, maybe manuals helped spread medical knowledge.

D Answers will vary. Correct answer: a

⌂ 2.05 Have students read the passage individually, or play the audio and have students read along.

OVERVIEW OF THE READING

The passage introduces medical pioneer Al-Zahrawi, who worked for the Spanish royal family in Córdoba in the 12th century. Al-Zahrawi invented a number of surgical instruments, some of which still look familiar today. He also made effort to research and record as much about medical treatments at the time as possible, compiling his knowledge in a 30-volume collection known as *Al-Tasrif*. After the manual was nearly destroyed, it was eventually translated and became an important work taught for centuries in medical schools.

Online search terms: Al-Zahrawi, Al-Tasrif, The Method of Medicine

 UNDERSTANDING THE READING
(pages 178–179)

A Summarizing

Students are asked to complete a summary of the passage.

- Have students work individually to complete the activity. Allow them to refer to the passage if needed.
- Check answers as a class. Discuss where students found the answers.

B Identifying Main Ideas

Students are asked to match each section from the passage to its main idea.

- Have students complete the activity individually before checking answers in pairs.
- Check answers as a class.

C Critical Thinking: Inferring Purpose

The *Critical Thinking* box explains how to infer an author's purpose by looking at clues in the language used. Some examples of purpose include: to entertain, to inform, and to persuade. For this exercise, students analyze Paragraphs A–C to determine the author's purpose.

- Get students to reread the opening paragraphs.
- Have them work in pairs to complete the exercise.
- Discuss as a class. Do students think that the opening is effective? If so, why? If not, what do they suggest as a better option?

D Sequencing

Students are asked to put the events in order to complete a timeline of events in Al-Zahrawi's life and achievements.

- Have students work individually to complete the activity. Encourage students to scan the passage to find the information quickly.
- Check answers as a class. Ask students where they found the answers.

E Understanding Details

Students are asked to answer questions relating to Al-Zahrawi's work *Al-Tasrif*. For item **1**, note that answers may vary.

- Have students work individually or in pairs to complete the activity.
- Check answers as a class.

F Critical Thinking: Reflecting

Students are asked to think about the significance of *Al-Tasrif* as well as other books that had an impact on science or society.

• Have students work alone to write notes before forming pairs or small groups to discuss.

• Discuss answers as a class. Ask for volunteers to share their opinions and reasons.

UNDERSTANDING THE READING

A **1.** Córdoba / Spain

2. royal court

3. pioneer

4. (medical) knowledge

5. surgery

B **1.** d (Explanation: *From his medical bag, he takes out a tool that he made himself—a pair of forceps with a semicircular end designed to pull the fetus from the mother.*)

2. e (Explanation: *During his long career, he compiled huge amounts of medical knowledge based on existing texts and his own experience.*)

3. b (Explanation: *This work was a 30-volume collection of all medical knowledge available at the time.*)

4. a (Explanation: *There was only a single handwritten copy of Al-Tasrif. It was almost lost during an attack on the area in 1010...*)

5. c (Explanation: *Al-Zahrawi's legacy can still be seen in many of the techniques and tools used in modern hospitals.*)

C **1.** b (See Paragraphs A–C.)

2. b (Explanation: Examples of verbs that appeared at the beginning of the passage are *is*, *has*, *sees*, and *takes*.)

3. c

D a, f, d, c, b, e

E Answers will vary. Possible answers:

1. treatment for head injuries / treatment for spinal injuries / techniques for amputating a limb / information about various surgical instruments and tools (See Paragraphs E–F.)

2. The book had the first ever pictures of surgical instruments. (See Paragraph F: *The work also includes the world's first illustrations of surgical instruments, such as knives, scissors, and forceps.*)

3. Catgut was used for sewing up a patient after surgery. It was useful because it dissolved naturally. (See Paragraph F: *One of Al-Zahrawi's most important inventions was the use of catgut for sewing up a patient internally after surgery. Catgut is a strong substance that can dissolve naturally in the body.*)

4. The only handwritten copy of *Al-Tasrif* was almost destroyed in an attack in 1010. (See Paragraph G: *There was only a single handwritten copy of Al-Tasrif. It was almost lost during an attack on the area in 1010, when many buildings and documents were destroyed.*)

5. After the text was translated into Latin and printed, its contents became more widely known. (See Paragraph H: *The printed translation spread Al-Zahrawi's knowledge throughout Europe.*)

F Answers will vary. Possible answers:

1. I think much of modern medicine would be different today, especially surgery and surgical tools.

2. Charles Darwin's book on evolution had a major impact on science as it explained natural selection and how species naturally evolve.

DEVELOPING READING SKILLS
(page 180)

Reading Skill: Understanding Passive Sentences

The *Reading Skill* box explains the difference between the active and passive voice. In a passive sentence, the focus is on the recipient of the action, and not the doer (agent) of the action. The passive voice is often used when the agent is unknown or already understood, or when the recipient of an action is the focus of the sentence. For example, in news articles, the passive voice is commonly used to draw attention to events rather than the people who did them (especially if the agents are unknown). However, passive sentences can sometimes include an agent, which is introduced with the preposition *by*.

A Identifying Passive Sentences

Students are asked to identify whether each sentence is active or passive.
- Have students work individually to complete the exercise.
- Have them form pairs to compare their answers.
- Check answers as a class.

B Understanding Passive Sentences

Students look at three passive sentences and identify the differences between them.
- Have students work individually to complete the exercise.
- Have them compare answers in pairs.
- Check answers as a class.

ANSWER KEY

DEVELOPING READING SKILLS

A 1. P
   2. A
   3. P
   4. A

B 1. b (Explanation: The agent is Al-Zahrawi.)
   2. a, c
   3. c (Explanation: The agents are most likely doctors and medical students.)
   4. a (Explanation: We can't infer the agent(s) from the context.)

Video

VIEWING: HEALTHCARE INNOVATOR *(pages 181–182)*

Overview of the Video

The video features an interview with engineer and National Geographic Emerging Explorer Dr. Aydogan Ozcan, who is working on using cell phone technology to diagnose and improve the treatment of infectious diseases worldwide. In the interview, Dr. Ozcan demonstrates how a healthcare provider can use a cell phone to assist with a malaria diagnosis.

Online search terms: Aydogan Ozcan

BEFORE VIEWING

A Predicting

Students are asked to predict how cell phones might be useful for testing people's health.
- Have students study the title and caption, and discuss their ideas in pairs.
- Discuss as a class.

B Learning About the Topic

The paragraph prepares students for the video by providing them with some background information about infectious diseases and the challenges in treating them. Students then answer questions about the information in the paragraph.
- Have students read the paragraph individually.
- Have them work in pairs to share their ideas and make notes.
- Have a class discussion. Get students to share their answers. Also ask students if they know of any other infectious diseases that are a worldwide problem.

C Vocabulary in Context

This exercise introduces students to some of the key words used in the video. Students use context to deduce the meaning of the words.
- Have students work on the exercise individually.
- Have them form pairs to check their answers.
- Discuss as a class. Elicit example sentences for each word.

BEFORE VIEWING

A   Answers will vary. Possible answer:

Health apps on smartphones can help monitor a person's heart rate, quality of sleep, etc. which could be useful medical data.

B   not enough proper medical facilities located near people, medical treatment is too expensive for many people

C 1. monitor

  2. diagnose (Note: The noun form, *diagnosis*, is also commonly used.)

  3. process

WHILE VIEWING

A ▶ Understanding Main Ideas

Have students read the items before playing the video.
- Have them complete the task while the video is playing.
- Check answers as a class.

B ▶ Understanding Details

Have students read the steps and complete any that they remember from the first viewing before playing the video a second time.
- Play the video again. Have students complete the task while the video is playing.
- Check answers as a class.

WHILE VIEWING

A   1, 3, 4

B 1. attachment

  2. "malaria"

  3. (diagnostic) test

  4. user

  5. captures / processes

  6. result

     (Explanation: See video from 1:19)

AFTER VIEWING

A Reacting to the Video

Students are asked to think about other possible medical applications of cell phone technology.
- Allow time for students to brainstorm individually before discussing in pairs.
- Discuss as a class. Make a mind map of students' ideas on the board.

B Critical Thinking: Applying

Students are asked to think about how data on infectious diseases could be used.
- Allow time for students to discuss in pairs.
- Discuss as a class. Is it important to collect such data? How does the data help in dealing with infectious diseases?

AFTER VIEWING

A   Answers will vary. Possible answers:

Cell phones could help patients keep track of the medicine they take. / Patients could use their cell phones to take pictures of skin conditions or other symptoms and send these pictures to doctors at a hospital far away to get a preliminary diagnosis. / Doctors and patients could also stay in touch about care and maintenance for a disease using cell phones.

B   Answers will vary. Possible answers:

The data provided by the app could be used to trace outbreaks of an infectious disease, and help warn people. It could also be used to identify the most badly affected areas, and then direct aid organizations or medical volunteers to those specific locations to offer help.

Reading 2

PREPARING TO READ *(page 183)*

A Building Vocabulary

The paragraph contains seven key vocabulary items that appear in the reading passage. Students should use contextual clues to deduce the meaning of the words.

- Have students complete the task individually.
- Check answers as a class. Elicit example sentences for each vocabulary item.

B Building Vocabulary

The sentences in the box contain three key vocabulary items. Students should use contextual clues to deduce the meaning of the words.

- Have students work individually.
- Check answers as a class. Elicit example sentences for each vocabulary item.

See Vocabulary Extension 8 in the Student Book for additional practice with antonyms.

C Using Vocabulary

Students should use the new vocabulary items while discussing the question.

- Have students work in pairs to answer the question. If necessary, provide prompts to support their discussion.
- Check answers as a class. Elicit example answers from students.

D Predicting

Students are asked to read the title and headings and look at the photos to predict the topic of the reading passage.

- Allow time for students to skim the title and headings, and to look at the photos.
- Discuss as a class. Revisit this exercise after students have completed the reading.

2.06 Have students read the passage individually, or play the audio and have students read along.

OVERVIEW OF THE READING

The passage describes two areas of medical research where breakthroughs are happening. The first is regenerative medicine, which aims to create replacement body parts and organs from human tissue. The second is nanotechnology, where tiny nanoshells are being used to help in surgery as well as to treat cancer. The passage is based on the articles *Miracle Grow* by Josie Glausiusz and *Nano's Big Future* by Jennifer Kahn, both of which appeared in *National Geographic* magazine.

Online search terms: regenerative medicine, nanoshells, The Big Idea: Organ Regeneration, Nano's Big Future

UNDERSTANDING THE READING
(pages 187–188)

A Summarizing

Students complete a summary of the reading passage.

- Explain that students should use no more than two words in each space. Note that synonyms are possible for some answers.
- Have students work individually to complete the activity. Allow them to refer to the reading if necessary.
- Check answers as a class.

B Understanding Details

Students identify the benefits of regenerative medicine that are mentioned in the passage.

- Have students complete the exercise individually.
- Check answers as a class. Discuss where students found the relevant information.

C Understanding Details

Students complete a chart with information about the innovations mentioned in the reading.

- Have students work in pairs. Encourage them to scan the passage to find the relevant information.
- Check answers as a class.

D Sequencing

Students put the steps for growing a kidney in the correct order, based on the infographic in the passage.

- Allow students time to work individually.
- Check answers as a class.

E Inferring Meaning

Students first find and underline the words in the passage. Then they use context to deduce the meaning of the words. Lastly, they complete the definitions with their own words.

- Have students work in pairs to locate the words in the passage and deduce their meaning. Note that answers may vary slightly depending on wording.
- Check answers as a class.

F Understanding Referencing

Students are asked to identify the noun that each pronoun refers to.

- Have students work individually to complete the exercise.
- Check answers as a class. Remind students that pronouns are a useful tool for avoiding repetition in writing; however, the antecedent must always be clear.

G Critical Thinking: Synthesizing

Students compare two medical technologies discussed in the two reading passages.

- Have students work individually to note their ideas. Allow them time to review the information about catgut in Reading 1, if necessary.
- Have students discuss in pairs or in small groups.
- If time permits, discuss as a class.

ANSWER KEY

UNDERSTANDING THE READING

A
1. cells
2. prosthetics / (organ) transplants / body parts
3. experimental
4. human
5. nanoshells
6. leaking / leaking out
7. cancer
8. side effects

B   1, 3

C   **Scientist(s):** e, b, a, c, d

     Innovation: long-term; sheep; implant; blood vessels / arteries; healthy tissue

D a. 6

   b. 1

   c. 3

   d. 2

   e. 5

   f. 4

E   Answers will vary. Possible answers:

   1. improved / made it better

   2. isn't a lot / is not enough / is too little

   3. phrase it differently / describe it differently / say it using different words / rephrase it / reword it

   4. join them / put them back together / connect them together again

F **1.** These parts

   2. donor organs

   3. doctors

   4. nanoshells

G   Both catgut and nanoshells can be used in surgeries to sew up patients internally.

Writing

OVERVIEW

In this section, students learn how to write a research-based essay. The lesson starts by teaching students how to effectively evaluate information found online, and then explains how to quote and cite sources based on APA Style. In the *Writing Task*, students apply these lessons by writing and revising an essay about an innovation in the field of medicine, science, or technology. Students begin with a brainstorming and research exercise, before selecting the best ideas and organizing them in an outline. Students then draft their essays, improve their drafts, and correct common mistakes related to in-text citations.

 EXPLORING WRITTEN ENGLISH
(pages 189–191)

Writing Skill: Evaluating Information Online

The *Writing Skill* box provides some guidelines and points to think about when evaluating information found online. Students need to be aware that some websites contain inaccurate or unreliable information. Some factors to take into consideration when evaluating an online source are: a site's overall purpose or motivation, how recent the information is, the authority of the source, and whether any important information is left out.

A Critical Thinking: Evaluating Sources

Students look at a list of sources and their descriptions and decide how reliable each one is. This exercise is to be done after going over the information in the *Writing Skill* box.

- Have students complete the task individually before sharing ideas with a partner. Note that students' rankings may vary slightly.
- Ask partners to share their reasons for assigning each ranking.
- Discuss as a class. Ask students to share the reasons for their rankings.

Ideas for … EXPANSION

Have students work in small groups to find an example of a website that provides medical advice or information. They are to evaluate the website and decide whether it is a reliable source of information. They can use the information in the *Writing Skill* box to help them. Ask each group to present their site to the class and explain their evaluation. Ask the class to say whether they agree with the evaluation.

Language for Writing: Introduction to Quoting and Citing Sources

The *Language for Writing* box introduces some basic guidelines for citing websites when using direct quotes. The citation style covered in this unit is the APA Style. An in-text citation is one that occurs within an essay. The Reference section comes at the end of an essay and contains full citations of all the sources used. The information in the box also shows students how to fit a direct quote into a sentence. Go over the chart and highlight the placement of punctuation and the in-text citations.

See the Writing Citations section in the Independent Student Handbook of the Student Book for more information on citing print sources.

B Using Quotes

Students practice fitting a direct quote into a sentence grammatically.
- Have students complete the activity individually.
- Have students form pairs to compare answers.
- Check answers as a class.

C Using Quotes

Students choose which part of the quote to use in each sentence.
- Tell students to pay attention to the grammatical structure of the sentence when choosing the part of the quote.
- Have students complete the activity individually.
- Have students form pairs to compare answers.
- Check answers as a class.

D Citing Sources

Students correct errors in in-text citations. Encourage students to use the information in the *Language for Writing* box to complete the activity. (Note that the online references have been created for this activity; they are not actual URLs.)
- Have students work in pairs to complete the activity.
- Check answers as a class.

EXPLORING WRITTEN ENGLISH
WRITING SKILL

A Answers will vary. Possible answers:

a. 4 (Explanation: It's a newspaper, but readers should beware since it has a political leaning. Also, its focus is not specifically on medicine or nutrition.)

b. 3 (Explanation: While it's good to get a professional's opinion, a blog is often not fact-checked in the way that a newspaper is, so blogs can be a source of misinformation.)

c. 2 (Explanation: The information is not very up-to-date, but the source is reliable and has no other purpose other than informing the public.)

d. 1 (Explanation: The site is trustworthy and up to date, and its contributors are currently working in the field of medicine or nutrition.)

e. 5 (Explanation: The site's main purpose is to sell a product, so all the information on the site may be written to convince readers to buy the product.)

LANGUAGE FOR WRITING

B 1. a

2. b

3. a

C 1. "…understand urbanization in isolation from economic development."

2. "…possibilities for doing things that interest them."

3. "…were the first to disappear."

D 1. As Lampl **(n.d.)** explains…

2. According to *The Future of Diagnosis* **(2016)**…

3. …about their condition" (Maple, 2018, **para. 10**).

WRITING TASK *(page 192)*

A Brainstorming

Read the *Goal* box aloud so students are familiar with the writing task before brainstorming. The aim of the essay is to introduce a recent innovation, and to talk about its importance. The brainstorming task focuses first on listing innovations that students know about.

- Have students work in pairs or in small groups. Students can list innovations that are in this unit or ones that they know based on their own background knowledge.
- Discuss as a class. Get groups to share their ideas.

B Planning

Students decide on an innovation from their brainstorming notes and complete the outline for their essays.

- Allow students to do some additional online research. Tell them to find reliable sources from which they can use relevant direct quotes. Remind them to note the reference information for each source so they can cite it in their essays.
- Allow students time to complete their outlines individually. Provide assistance as needed.

C First Draft

Have students write a first draft of their essays based on their outline.

- Remind students to cite sources in their essay and to provide a reference entry for each one at the end of the essay. Get them to refer to the *Language for Writing* box if needed.
- Allow students time to complete the task individually. Provide assistance as needed. Refrain from error correction at this point.

ANSWER KEY

WRITING TASK

A Answers will vary. Possible answers:

regenerative body replacements and organs, nanoshells for surgery and cancer treatment, cell phone technology for malaria and tuberculosis

B Answers will vary. Possible answers:

Innovation: Aydogan Ozcan's cell phone technology for infectious disease diagnosis

Thesis Statement: Ozcan and his research team have developed a way to turn regular cell phones into diagnostic tools.

Body Paragraphs

Topic Sentence 1: Ozcan's invention is important because it is very accurate and easy to use.

Details: Not reliant on trained healthcare workers, scans can be sent to a central hospital

Topic Sentence 2: Another reason that Ozcan's invention is important is that it is inexpensive.

Details: only need cell phone and Internet connection; $10 of hardware, possibly even cheaper in future

Concluding Paragraph

Summary Statement: By making use of existing technology—cell phones—Ozcan and his team have invented a medical tool that is accurate and easy to use.

Final Thought: Ozcan's simple tool might one day save the lives of millions of people all over the world.

REVISING PRACTICE *(page 193)*

The *Revising Practice* box contains an exercise that demonstrates several ways students can improve their first drafts.

- Allow students time to analyze the draft and complete the exercise. Note that this essay is based on the work of Aydogan Ozcan, the engineer featured in the unit's video.
- Check answers as a class. Ask students to identify each change and explain how it makes the revised draft stronger.

D Revised Draft

Students should apply the revision techniques used in the *Revising Practice* box to their own drafts, where applicable.

- Explain to students that they will be using the questions as a guide for checking and improving their drafts.
- As a class, go over the questions carefully to make sure students understand them.
- Allow students time to revise their essays.

EDITING PRACTICE

The *Editing Practice* box trains students to spot and correct common errors related to writing sentences containing direct quotes. As a class, go over the information in the box carefully to make sure students understand what to look out for.

- Allow students time to complete the exercise individually.
- Check answers as a class by asking students to read their corrected sentences aloud and explain the errors.

ANSWER KEY

REVISING PRACTICE

1. b, a, c
2. **d.** This turns the cell phone into **a** "mobile medical lab with the capability to test and diagnose diseases" (Ward, 2012).

   e. As Eisenberg **(2009)** points out, ...

EDITING PRACTICE

1. Lampl (2017) points out that a 3-D-printed hand costs 40 pounds, or about <u>the</u> "same price as an adult ticket for a ride on the London Eye" (para. 10).

2. Root (2018) believes that health workers need to calm down patients who <u>have</u> "read too much about medical conditions online" (para. 4).

3. Science blogger Anna Chung (2018) says that regenerative medicine <u>has</u> "completely changed the game" when it comes to organ transplantation (para. 7).

4. According to *What's New in Medicine* (n.d.), research shows that "~~even though~~ about 99.9 percent of the DNA between two individuals is identical" (para. 1).

E Final Draft

Have students apply the skills taught in *Editing Practice* to their own revised drafts and check for any other errors.

- Allow students time to edit their drafts.
- Walk around and monitor students as they work. Provide assistance as needed.
- Collect students' work once they have completed it.
- For the next class, show anonymous examples of good essays and common errors.

> ### Ideas for ... EXPANSION
>
> Have students work in groups of three to help review and edit each other's essays further. Ask each student to read another group member's essays and do the following:
> - Correct one error in grammar, spelling, etc.
> - Give one compliment.
> - Give one piece of feedback to help improve the essay.
>
> Allow students time to read each other's essays, take notes, and then discuss their feedback.

 UNIT REVIEW

Students can work in groups on this recap of the unit. For question **1**, encourage students to use the target vocabulary words when appropriate. For questions **2** and **3**, encourage them to check the relevant pages of the unit for answers.

- Allow students time to form groups to answer the three questions.
- Ask each group to present its answer for question **1**.

WORLD LANGUAGES

9

ACADEMIC TRACK

Anthropology / Linguistics

ACADEMIC SKILLS

READING	Understanding predictions
WRITING	Planning an essay using a T-chart
GRAMMAR	Presenting counterarguments
CRITICAL THINKING	Applying ideas

UNIT OVERVIEW

This unit focuses on languages. Students learn about language families, the changing role of English, as well as the issue of dying languages. Additionally, the unit describes the efforts being made to record the history and culture of speakers of languages that are dying out.

- **READING 1:** English is one of the world's most commonly spoken languages. Its future role in global society, however, may change.

- **VIDEO:** A group of researchers are on a mission to preserve the world's dying languages.

- **READING 2:** When a language dies out, it's more than a loss of words; it's a loss of historical, cultural, and scientific knowledge.

Students draw on what they have read and watched to write a persuasive essay about whether everyone should speak the same language. The unit prepares them for the writing task by introducing vocabulary for talking about language-related issues, and by teaching them how to identify expressions for making predictions. Students are then taught how to plan an essay using a T-chart, and introduced to language for making counterarguments. Finally, the unit takes students through the steps of brainstorming and planning, and shows them how to revise and edit their essays.

 THINK AND DISCUSS *(page 195)*

The photo is of the Signpost Forest in Canada, which has a large collection of signs from different places. The title and questions help prepare students for the subject matter covered in the unit.

- Have students study the picture, title, and caption.
- Discuss the photo as a class. What does this picture show? Do students recognize any of the languages? Can they read any of the signs?
- Discuss the questions as a class. For question **1**, ask students to name the languages they speak and rank how well they speak each language on a scale of 1 to 5, with 5 being "fluent".

ANSWER KEY

THINK AND DISCUSS

Answers will vary. Possible answers:

1. I speak three languages. We speak Arabic at home, which is my native language, but at work I use English, which I am proficient in but not completely fluent yet. As a student, I learned Malay in school, which I can speak conversationally.

2. The most common languages in my country are Malay, English, Mandarin, Tamil, and Hindi.

 EXPLORE THE THEME *(pages 196–197)*

The opening spread shows a map of the major language families in the world today, and information about the decreasing number of languages. The three main families are Indo-European, Afro-Asiatic, and Sino-Tibetan, but there are many more families that make up the 7,000 languages spoken in the world.

- Allow time for students to study the spread and work in pairs to answer the questions.
- Check answers as a class. For question **2**, ask students to give reasons for their ideas. For question **3**, tell students to support their opinions with examples or reasons. Note that students' opinions about question **3** may change after they complete the unit. Revisit the question after completing the unit if there is time.
- Elicit example sentences from students for each blue word.

ANSWER KEY

EXPLORE THE THEME

A **1.** Indo-European is the largest language family. Languages in this family are spoken in places such as North and South America and Europe.

2. Answers will vary. Possible answer: The "other" areas are home to indigenous languages that only small populations speak. These languages are not part of one of the major language families.

3. Answers will vary. Possible answers: As the world globalizes, more people are moving permanently from rural to urban areas. As a result, languages such as Mandarin or English are becoming the common everyday languages used in cities, which means local languages are disappearing because not enough people use them. Although our linguistic diversity is being reduced, more people are now able to communicate with one another as they speak the global languages.

B considerably; linguistic; constitute

Reading 1

PREPARING TO READ *(page 198)*

A Building Vocabulary

The paragraph is about the benefits of being multilingual, which is discussed in the reading passage. It contains seven key vocabulary items that appear in the passage. Students should use contextual clues to deduce the meaning of the words.

- Have students work individually to complete the exercise.
- Check answers as a class. Elicit example sentences for each vocabulary item.

See Vocabulary Extension 9 in the Student Book for additional practice with adjective + language.

B Using Vocabulary

Students should use the new vocabulary items while discussing the questions.

- Have students work in pairs to answer the questions. Ask them to share their own personal experiences with language learning in the discussion when appropriate. If necessary, provide some prompts to help with their discussion.
- Check answers as a class. Elicit example responses from students.

C Brainstorming

Students are asked to think about the English language and its importance in the future.

- Have students work in pairs or in small groups to brainstorm ideas together.
- Allow groups time to discuss their answers.
- Discuss answers as a class. Elicit opinions and ideas from each group.

D Predicting

Students are asked to skim the title and subheadings, and look at the photos to predict the topic of the passage.

- Allow students time to look at the title and subheadings. If necessary, elicit or explain the meaning of *multilingualism* (speaking multiple, or more than two, languages).
- Have students work individually. Tell them to check their ideas as they read the passage.

PREPARING TO READ

A 1. lead to

    2. acquire

    3. furthermore

    4. competence

    5. expand

    6. anticipate

    7. native

B Answers will vary. Possible answers:

    1. I think reading is the best way to first learn a language. When you read, you acquire new vocabulary all the time. It's good for developing basic competence.

    2. Being able to speak a second language is a useful skill that can lead to better job opportunities.

C Answers will vary. Possible answers:

    1. English is the language of business, so many people learn it to find jobs.

    2. It might still be important, but other languages such as Mandarin might also be widely spoken.

D Answers will vary. Correct answer: a

🎧 **2.07** Have students read the passage individually, or play the audio and have students read along.

OVERVIEW OF THE READING

The passage is about the new linguistic order that is emerging in the world, and the status of English in the future. As the global population continues to rise, the growth—especially in developing countries—is shifting the world's language landscape. There are currently more speakers of Chinese than English, and while English is still the largest second language, this reality will likely shift over the next 50 years. However, English is likely to retain its place as the dominant language of science, and perhaps as one of the main languages for business. The passage content is based on the article *English in Decline as a First Language, Study Says*, which appeared on National Geographic News.

Online search terms: David Graddol, English in Decline as a First Language, Study Says, the future of English

UNDERSTANDING THE READING
(pages 202–203)

A Understanding Main Ideas

Students are asked to match each main idea to a paragraph.

- Have students read through the main ideas in the exercise first.
- Then allow them to complete the activity individually.
- Check answers as a class.

B Understanding Details

Students scan the passage to answer questions about the details in the passage.

- Allow time for students to go back to the reading.
- Check answers as a class. Discuss where students found the answers.

C Inferring Meaning

Students first find and underline the words in the passage. Then they use context to deduce the meaning of the words. Lastly, they complete the definitions.

- Have students work individually to locate the words in the passage and deduce their meaning.
- Check answers as a class. Elicit example sentences for each word.

D Interpreting Visual Information

Students answer questions related to content in the graph in the reading passage.

- Have students work individually to complete the activity.
- Check answers as a class.
- If time permits, discuss the data in the graph. Which piece of information is surprising to students?

E Critical Thinking: Applying Ideas

The *Critical Thinking* box explains that applying your own experiences to ideas you read about can help deepen your understanding of the topic. When reading a persuasive essay, for example, considering your personal experiences helps you formulate your own opinion on the topic. For this exercise, students are asked to think about their own experiences with learning a second language, and their opinions about the importance of language study.

- Allow students time to think about the questions and write their answers individually.
- Have them work in pairs to discuss their answers.
- Discuss as a class.

UNDERSTANDING THE READING

A 1. G (Explanation: *Linguists anticipate that in the future, the majority of the world's population will speak more than one language. As a result, people who speak only one language may have a difficult time in a multilingual society.*)

2. D (Explanation: *… a separate study shows that English is expanding its dominance in the world of science.*)

3. F (Explanation: *At the same time, he notes, businesses will increasingly look for multilingual employees.*)

4. A (Explanation: *The world's population rose quickly during the second half of the 20th century, and much of this increase took place in developing countries. This has had an impact on the world's top languages.*)

5. C (Explanation: *However, according to Graddol, it is unlikely that one language will dominate in the near future.*)

6. E (Explanation: *"Because of its scale and dynamism," he says, "science has become the most active and dynamic creator of new language in the world today."*)

7. B (Explanation: *Currently, English still has the third largest number of speakers, with Arabic and Hindi lagging considerably behind in fourth and fifth places. However, these two languages are expected to catch up by around 2050.*)

B 1. in developing countries (See Paragraph A.)

2. Bengali, Tamil, Malay (See Paragraph B.)

3. It makes international collaboration and research easier, and publications can reach more people. (See Paragraph D.)

4. Mandarin Chinese is becoming a global business language because China's growing economy means that more businesses will need to have Chinese speakers. (See Paragraph F.)

C 1. a

2. b

3. b

4. b

D 1. Mandarin (greatest number) Spanish (second greatest number)

2. English

3. English and French. These languages are important in business, education, and daily life. (Note that these are not the only languages in the world that have more non-native speakers than native speakers.)

E Answers will vary. Possible answers:

1. I am studying English so that I can write academic essays in English and attend college overseas.

2. I think the more languages you learn, the better. It helps broaden your thinking and worldview when you learn another language. It also helps people in my country do business internationally. / No, I think it's better to learn two languages well than to be able to speak a little of a lot of languages. It's enough to be able to speak our native tongue and a global language. It's better to focus on fewer languages and master them.

DEVELOPING READING SKILLS
(page 204)

Reading Skill: Understanding Predictions

The *Reading Skill* box explains how to identify levels of certainty in predictions. The verb *will* is used to communicate the strongest level of certainty, while verbs like *expect*, *anticipate*, and *believe* indicate a slightly weaker but still reasonably strong level of certainty. When writers are not certain, words like *probably* and *seem* are used. And when writers are even less certain, modals such as *may*, *might*, and *could* are used.

A Identifying Predictions

Students are asked to identify predictions in the passage and their level of certainty.

• Have students work individually to complete the exercise.

• Have them form pairs to compare their answers.

• Check answers as a class.

B Analyzing Predictions

Students are asked to find predictions in the reading passage, identify their level of certainty, and give their opinions about each one.

- Have students work individually to complete item **1**.
- Have them form pairs to work on items **2** and **3**.
- Check answers as a class. For item **3**, have a class discussion if time permits.

ANSWER KEY

DEVELOPING READING SKILLS

A 1. expects (Explanation: *Montgomery expects that in the future, English will continue to expand its role in science, especially in international settings.*)

2. may (Explanation: *And English may not be the only language of business.*)

B 1. a. Paragraph C: *However, according to Graddol, it is unlikely that one language will dominate in the near future.*

b. Paragraph C: *As a result of these trends, Graddol says, "the status of English as a global language may peak soon."*

c. Paragraph F: *Businesses whose employees speak only one language will find themselves at a disadvantage.*

d. Paragraph G: *As a result, people who speak only one language may have a difficult time in a multilingual society.*

2. a. 2 (Explanation: *unlikely*)

b. 1 (Explanation: *may*)

c. 3 (Explanation: *will*)

d. 1 (Explanation: *may*)

3. Answers will vary. Possible answer:
Although Mandarin is becoming an important language, I don't think English is going to be replaced by other languages completely. I think it's likely that there will be a few global languages.

Video

VIEWING: ENDURING VOICES
(pages 205–206)

40 MINS

Overview of the Video

The video introduces the Enduring Voices Project by the Living Tongues Institute. The project aims to record as many dying languages around the world as possible. Researchers travel to remote locations to meet with people who speak traditional languages and to also teach them how to create a record of the languages. The video originally aired on National Geographic as *Enduring Voices Expeditions*.

Online search terms: Enduring Voices Project, the Living Tongues Institute, Enduring Voices Expeditions

BEFORE VIEWING

A Predicting

Students are asked to think about what is happening in the photo and the reasons for it.
- Have students study the title, photo, and caption and predict the situation shown in the photo.
- Discuss as a class.

B Learning About the Topic

The paragraph provides students with information related to the video content. Students then answer questions about the information in the paragraph.
- Have students read the paragraph individually.
- Have them work in pairs to answer the questions.
- Have a class discussion.

C Vocabulary in Context

This exercise introduces students to some of the key words used in the video. Students use context to deduce the meaning of the words.
- Have students work on the exercise individually.
- Check answers in pairs.
- Discuss as a class. Elicit example sentences for each word.

BEFORE VIEWING

A   Answers will vary. Correct answer:

The researchers are interviewing speakers of a language at risk of disappearing. They are trying to preserve the language and its cultural heritage by recording it.

B   **1.** They are trying to preserve the culture and history of these minority languages.

2. Answers will vary. Possible answer: English and Hindi are used more on TV and the Internet and are more useful for young people to get jobs.

C   **1.** diversity

2. neglect

3. abandon

4. extinction (Note: Students may be familiar with *extinction* as used to talk about animal species.)

WHILE VIEWING

A ▶ Understanding Main Ideas

Have students read the items before playing the video. Note that more than one answer may be possible for some.
- Have them complete the task while the video is playing.
- Check answers as a class.

B ▶ Understanding Details

Have students write any answers they recall from the first viewing before playing the video a second time.
- Play the video again. Have students complete the task while the video is playing.
- Check answers as a class.

WHILE VIEWING

A   **1.** Australia

2. the last speaker

3. elders / village elders / the older generation

4. record / recording

B   **1.** T (Explanation: *This time, they are in the extreme northeast of India, a remote area bordering Bhutan, Myanmar, and China. It's considered a language "hot spot" ...*)

2. NG (Explanation: No reason is given as to why they prefer to speak English and Hindi.)

3. F (Explanation: In the video, the researchers interviewed a family who could speak Apatani.)

4. T (Explanation: *... the team trains local people to use special language technology kits.*)

AFTER VIEWING

A Reacting to the Video

Students are asked to think about whether the efforts of the Enduring Voices team are sufficient to preserve dying languages.
- Allow time for students to think about the questions individually before forming pairs to discuss.
- Discuss as a class. What do students think it means for a language to be alive?

B Critical Thinking: Synthesizing

Students are asked to compare the language trend shown in the video (disappearing languages, younger people not speaking traditional languages, etc.) with the predictions in the first reading, and see if they relate to one another.
- Allow time for students to review Reading 1 before forming pairs to discuss.
- Discuss as a class.

AFTER VIEWING

A   Answers will vary. Possible answers:

I think it's a start. If a language is recorded and written down, at least there's some record of it. / I don't think it's enough. Even if words and phrases are recorded, a language is not really alive if no one is using it.

B   Answers will vary. Possible answer:

In the video, we saw that younger people tend to speak English or Hindi, instead of Apatani. This supports the trends mentioned in Reading 1 about English being a global language and Hindi as a growing language.

Reading 2

  PREPARING TO READ *(page 207)*

A Building Vocabulary

The exercise introduces ten key vocabulary items that appear in the reading passage. Students should first use a dictionary to check the definition of the words before using them to complete the sentences.

- Have students complete the task individually.
- Check answers as a class. Elicit example sentences for each vocabulary item.

B Using Vocabulary

Students should use the new vocabulary items while discussing the questions.

- Have students work in pairs to share their ideas. If necessary, provide prompts to support their discussion.
- Discuss as a class. Elicit example responses from students.

C Predicting

Students are asked to read the headings in the passage and discuss possible answers to them.

- Allow time for students to read the headings before discussing in pairs. Tell them to rely on what they have read in the unit so far as well as any background knowledge they have on the subject when writing their answers.
- Discuss as a class. Revisit this exercise after students have completed the reading.

ANSWER KEY

PREPARING TO READ

A 1. combined

2. rate, roughly, died out

3. critically

4. express, highly, rapidly

5. perspective

6. political

B Answers will vary. Possible answers:

1. People also express themselves through body language such as gestures or facial expressions. / Singing is a way of expressing your feelings.

2. I think the best way to learn a new language rapidly is to move to a place where the language is used in everyday life.

C Answers will vary. Correct answers:

How do languages die? When dominant languages like English are spoken even in remote areas, fewer and fewer people speak the local language, and eventually children stop learning the language altogether.

Why should we be concerned? Different languages offer different ways of looking at the world, and when they become extinct, we lose these different perspectives along with the cultural, historical, and even scientific knowledge that come with them.

How can we save dying languages? We can begin by documenting and recording these languages.

2.08 Have students read the passage individually, or play the audio and have students read along.

OVERVIEW OF THE READING

The passage explores the issue of language death and discusses the importance of preserving dying languages. It argues that with language loss, we lose the cultural, historical, and scientific information associated with the languages. The passage also explains how the Enduring Voices Project is trying to record these languages before they die out. We never know when knowledge embedded in these languages may help people in the present or future, so preserving these traditional languages is a service to both past and future generations.

Online search terms: language death, language hot spots, Enduring Voices Project

  UNDERSTANDING THE READING *(pages 211–212)*

A Understanding Main Ideas

Students answer questions about the main idea of each section. Note that this exercise corresponds to exercise **C** in the *Preparing to Read* section.

- Have students work individually to complete the activity. Allow them time to refer to the reading if necessary.
- Check answers as a class. Ask students to compare these answers to their predictions from the *Preparing to Read* section.

B Understanding Details

Students answer questions about details in the reading.
- Have students work individually to complete the exercise.
- Allow them time to skim the reading for the answers.
- Check answers as a class. Discuss where students found the relevant information.

C Interpreting Visual Information

Students answer questions about the map in the passage.
- Have students work in pairs to answer the questions.
- Check answers as a class. For question **3**, ask volunteers to share their thoughts.

D Understanding Effects

Students use details from the reading to complete a mind map about the effects of language loss.
- Have students work in pairs. Allow students time to look for the information in the passage.
- Check answers as a class. Discuss where in the reading students found the relevant information.

E Understanding Certainty

Students practice identifying levels of certainty in predictions, which they learned earlier in the unit.
- Have students work individually. Note that this is a two-part exercise. Students look for the predictions in the reading passage before they identify the words that express the level of certainty.
- Check answers as a class.

F Critical Thinking: Analyzing Arguments

Students read three counterarguments and decide which one is the strongest.
- Review what a counterargument is, if necessary.
- Have students work in pairs. Point out that the counterargument they choose may vary.
- Ask each pair to brainstorm some other possible counterarguments.
- If time permits, discuss as a class. Ask some pairs to share their additional counterargument.

UNDERSTANDING THE READING

A **1.** b

2. a

3. a

B **1.** They predict that over half of the world's languages will die out. (See Paragraph B.)

2. more powerful languages dominate; children choose to speak the dominant languages instead of their native languages; governments require the use of dominant languages (See Paragraphs C and D.)

3. They are changing attitudes. / They are recording cultural and historical information. / They are preserving important information for future generations.

C **1.** b

2. Northwest America, Central South America, Central and Eastern Siberia, Northern Australia

3. Answers will vary. Possible answers: All of these places have a powerful dominant language that is used in schools and in work life. / Some of the places are remote and their populations may be shrinking.

D **1.** cultural   **8.** dark green

2. numbers   **9.** skills

3. no words   **10.** Seri

4. color   **11.** desert

5. green   **12.** sailors

6. blue   **13.** maps

7. purple   **14.** modern equipment

E **1.** Paragraph B: *According to linguists, within the next century, nearly half of the world's current languages* **will** *disappear…*

2. Paragraph F: … *we* **might** *lose important scientific knowledge*

3. Paragraph G: …, *we* **may** *lose knowledge about plants that could someday lead to useful drugs / We* **may** *also lose information about the history and skills…*

F Answers will vary. Possible answer: 2

Additional counterargument: It's not a real language anymore if we only have a record of the language with no speakers actively using it.

Writing

OVERVIEW

In this section, students write a persuasive essay. The lesson starts by teaching how to brainstorm ideas using a T-chart, as well as how to present counterarguments. In the *Writing* task, students apply these lessons by writing and revising an essay that argues for or against having a single global language. Students begin with a brainstorming exercise before selecting the best ideas and organizing them in an outline. Students then draft their essays, improve their drafts, and correct common mistakes related to language for introducing counterarguments.

 EXPLORING WRITTEN ENGLISH
(pages 213–215)

Writing Skill: Planning an Essay Using a T-Chart

The *Writing Skill* box introduces how to use a T-chart when brainstorming ideas and planning an essay. A T-chart is an easy way to organize a list of pros and cons while considering ideas to write about in an essay. The T-chart should have details such as facts, statistics, or quotes to support the main ideas. Note that besides T-charts, students can also use other kinds of visual organizers for planning their essays.

A Completing a T-chart

Students use the information listed to complete the T-chart. This exercise is to be done after going over the information in the *Writing Skill* box.
- Explain that students should identify the main arguments (pros and cons) first, and then add the details.
- Have students complete the task individually before forming pairs to check their answers. Tell them to discuss some additional ideas as well.
- Check answers as a class. Elicit additional ideas that students discussed.

B Using a T-chart

Students practice brainstorming about a topic using a T-chart. Note that they are not asked to add any details.
- Have students work in pairs to complete the activity.
- Check answers as a class. Elicit ideas for pros and cons from each pair.

C Noticing

Students read a sentence and identify the argument and counterargument presented. This exercise is to be done before reading the *Language for Writing* box.
- Have students complete the activity individually.
- Have students compare answers in pairs.
- Check answers as a class.

Language for Writing: Presenting Counterarguments

The *Language for Writing* box explains how to introduce counterarguments in writing. Presenting the opposite side of an argument makes the main argument stronger. However, language choice is important when presenting a counterargument. Weaker modals like *may* and *might* are used for counterarguments, while stronger modals like *must*, *have*, and *should* are used for the main arguments. In addition, concession terms like *although*, *even though*, and *while* are often used to introduce a counterargument.

D Analyzing Arguments

Students analyze the language used in exercise **C**. Encourage students to refer to the information in the *Language for Writing* box as they complete the activity.
- Have students work individually to complete the activity.
- Check answers as a class.

E Presenting Counterarguments

Students practice presenting counterarguments by combining the ideas given. Note that answers will vary for this exercise.
- Have students work individually to complete the activity.
- Have students compare answers in pairs.
- Check answers as a class.

F Writing a Counterargument

Students use the content from exercise **B** to make a sentence containing an argument and counterargument.
- Have students work individually to complete the activity.
- Have them form pairs to share their answers.
- Discuss as a class. Elicit example sentences from volunteers.

EXPLORING WRITTEN ENGLISH

WRITING SKILL

A   **Pros:**

Idea 1: Important in media

Detail: over 500 mil. native English Internet users (Internet World Stats)

Idea 2: Important in science

Detail: 90% of scientific lit. is in Eng. (Montgomery)

Answers will vary. Possible answer:

Idea 3: Important in business

Cons:

Idea 1: English declining as 1st language

Detail: Eng. as 1st lang. will be spoken by only 5% of pop. in 2050 (Graddol)

Idea 2: Mandarin becoming more important

Detail: 898 mil. native Mandarin speakers; Eng. only 372 mil.

Answers will vary. Possible answer:

Idea 3: may lead to loss of cultural identity if one's native language is abandoned

B   Answers will vary. Possible answers:

Pros:

Young children are able to adapt to new languages more easily than adults.

Second-language learning can be done more naturally at a young age.

Cons:

It's expensive for parents to pay for second-language education starting in preschool.

Learning a second language and native language at the same time might be confusing for a child.

C 1. Argument 1: It's difficult for immigrant children to be bilingual.

Argument 2: Parents should encourage children to be bilingual.

2. Argument 2

LANGUAGE FOR WRITING

D 1. Although

2. should

E   Answers will vary. Possible answers:

1. Although English might be useful in some situations, most children should learn Mandarin as a second language.

2. While Mandarin may be difficult to learn, it is useful in the world of business.

3. Even though language diversity can lead to misunderstanding or conflict, we must preserve smaller languages because of the important knowledge they contain.

F   Answers will vary. Possible answer:

Although learning a second language may seem confusing for the child, children are actually able to acquire languages quickly and easily.

WRITING TASK *(page 216)*

A Brainstorming

Remind students that brainstorming is a useful first step for gathering ideas before writing, and that a T-chart is especially useful when thinking of arguments and counterarguments. Read the *Goal* box aloud so students are familiar with the writing task before brainstorming. The aim of the essay is to write a persuasive argument on whether everyone in the world should speak the same language. Students think about arguments for both sides of the topic in this step.

• Have students work in pairs or in small groups. Tell them to use a T-chart to help them.

• Discuss ideas as a class. Have students add their ideas to a large T-chart on the board.

B Planning

Students choose the side of the issue they want to write about and complete the outline for their essays.

• Encourage students to use details (facts, quotes, statistics) from the information in the unit. If necessary, allow them time to gather additional support online. Instruct students to note the citation information of each source they use.

• Allow students time to complete their outlines individually. Provide assistance as needed.

C First Draft

Have students write a first draft of their essays based on their outline.

- Remind students to cite sources and to have a Reference section at the end of the essay as they learned in Unit 8.
- Allow students time to complete the task individually. Provide assistance as needed. Refrain from error correction at this point.

ANSWER KEY

WRITING TASK

A Answers will vary. Possible answers:

Agree: communication problems will be eliminated, people of different backgrounds can work and live together, global business will be made easier

Disagree: cultural diversity may be threatened, smaller languages will die out, people will forget their histories and heritages, we will lose untranslated words and concepts

B Answers will vary. Possible answers:

Thesis Statement: Language diversity keeps us respectful of each other's differences and keeps our brains active, which is why a single global language is not necessary.

Body Paragraphs

Topic Sentence 1: We learn about how varied the cultures and people of the planet are through our languages.

Details: language is connected to culture, history; half the world's languages are disappearing, and having a single global language speeds up language loss, etc.

Counterargument 1: Even though a world where everyone speaks one language may seem convenient, …

Concluding Paragraph

Summary Statement: A world where people speak many languages is more respectful and supportive of different ways of life.

Final Thought: Effective communication is about more than just speaking the same language; it's about being open to hearing what others have to say.

REVISING PRACTICE *(page 217)*

The *Revising Practice* box contains an exercise that demonstrates several ways students can improve their first drafts.

- Allow students time to analyze the draft and complete the exercise. Note that this essay is a persuasive essay, but on a different topic to the writing task.
- Check answers as a class. Ask students to identify each change and explain how it makes the revised draft stronger.

D Revised Draft

Students should apply the revision techniques used in the *Revising Practice* box to their own drafts, where applicable.

- Explain to students that they will be using the questions as a guide for checking and improving their drafts.
- As a class, go over the questions carefully to make sure students understand them.
- Allow students time to revise their essays.

EDITING PRACTICE

The *Editing Practice* box trains students to spot and correct common errors related to using concession words and modals for introducing counterarguments.

- Allow students time to complete the exercise individually.
- Check answers as a class by asking students to read their corrected sentences aloud and explain the errors.

ANSWER KEY

REVISING PRACTICE

1. c, a, b
2. **d.** Even though an employee <u>may/might perform</u> their job well, it does not mean …

   e. Sentence to cross out: Studies also show that people have a harder time learning to play an instrument when they are older.

   f. <u>Although</u> some language learning programs promise fluency …

EDITING PRACTICE

1. While language instruction may <u>be</u> expensive, it is important that children learn a second language in order to compete in the global economy.
2. Even though Mandarin may soon become an important world language, <u>it</u> probably will be challenging for learners to learn its writing system.
3. Although French was an important language in the <u>past,</u> it shouldn't be an official UN language; there are just too few native speakers.

E Final Draft

Have students apply the skills taught in *Editing Practice* to their own revised drafts and check for any other errors.

- Allow students time to edit their drafts.
- Walk around and monitor students as they work. Provide assistance as needed.
- Collect students' work once they have completed it.
- For the next class, show anonymous examples of good essays and common errors.

Ideas for ... EXPANSION

Have students work in groups of three to help review and edit each other's essays further. Ask each student to read another group member's essays and do the following:

- Correct one error in grammar, spelling, etc.
- Give one compliment.
- Give one piece of feedback to help improve the essay.

Allow students time to read each other's essays, take notes, and then discuss their feedback.

UNIT REVIEW

Students can work in groups on this recap of the unit. For question **1**, encourage students to use the target vocabulary words when appropriate. For questions **2** and **3**, encourage them to check the relevant pages of the unit for answers.

- Allow students time to answer the questions in groups.
- Ask each group to present its answer for question **1**.

SURVIVAL INSTINCT

ACADEMIC TRACK
Psychology

ACADEMIC SKILLS
READING   Identifying adverbial phrases
WRITING   Writing a descriptive narrative essay
GRAMMAR   Using past forms for narratives
CRITICAL THINKING   Interpreting figurative language

UNIT OVERVIEW

This unit explores dangerous situations and people who survived them. Students learn how breathing can help control the body's fear response, and what to do when encountering dangerous animals in the wild. They will also read a number of survival stories of individuals faced with life-or-death situations.

- **READING 1:** An account of a climb on the treacherous K2 mountain highlights how the team members handled the challenge.

- **VIDEO:** Do you know what to do when a shark attacks you or an elephant charges at you? Take this survival quiz to find out.

- **READING 2:** Breathing is one of the best ways to deal with fear; one woman's story shows how it helped her live through a harrowing accident.

Students draw upon what they have read and watched to write a descriptive narrative essay about someone who overcame a difficult situation. The unit prepares them for the writing task by introducing vocabulary for talking about fear and risky situations, and by teaching them to identify adverbial phrases. Students then review past forms of verbs, and learn about the elements of a descriptive narrative. Finally, the unit takes students through the steps of brainstorming and planning, and shows them how to revise and edit their essays.

 THINK AND DISCUSS *(page 219)*

The photo shows a bear attempting to get to a man in a tree. The title and questions help prepare students for the subject matter covered in the unit.
- Have students study the picture, title, and caption.
- Discuss the photo as a class. Do they think the man made the right decision to go up the tree? What would students do in a similar situation?
- Discuss the questions as a class. For question **1**, ask students to share any survival stories that they know. For question **2**, have the class brainstorm a list of characteristics of people who are likely to survive dangerous situations.

ANSWER KEY

THINK AND DISCUSS

Answers will vary. Possible answers:
1. My parents were in a car accident. The car actually flipped over, but no one was hurt. They were very lucky.
2. people who don't panic, people who keep thinking positively, people who have been trained for dangerous situations, etc.

 EXPLORE THE THEME *(pages 220–221)*

The opening spread is about K2, the second highest mountain in the world. With its steep slopes and dangerous weather conditions, K2 is one of the deadliest mountains to climb in the world. It has only been successfully climbed a few hundred times. And twenty percent of those who have tried have sadly died on the mountain.
- Allow time for students to study the spread and answer the questions individually.
- Check answers as a class. For question **3**, explain the meaning of *savage* after students share their answers.
- Elicit example sentences from students for each blue word.

Reading 1

30 MINS PREPARING TO READ *(page 222)*

A Building Vocabulary

The paragraphs are a narrative about a mountain climbing trip in Myanmar, which is related to the topic of mountain climbing in the reading passage. They contain seven vocabulary items that appear in the passage. Students should use contextual clues to deduce the meaning of the words.

- Have students work individually to complete the exercise.
- Check answers as a class. Elicit example sentences for each vocabulary item.

B Using Vocabulary

Students should use the new vocabulary items while discussing the questions.

- Have students work in pairs to answer the questions. Ask them to share their own experiences or background knowledge if they have any. If necessary, provide some prompts to help with their discussion.
- Discuss as a class. Elicit example answers from students.

C Skimming

Students are asked to skim the passage to identify the type of text it is.

- Have students work individually to skim the passage and answer the question before sharing their answer with a partner.
- Tell them to check their ideas later as they read the passage.

2.09 Have students read the passage individually, or play the audio and have students read along.

OVERVIEW OF THE READING

The passage tells the story of a mountaineering team led by Gerlinde Kaltenbrunner and Ralf Dujmovits, and their attempt to summit K2 on the mountain's more treacherous side. Partway through the climb, Ralf turned back, but Gerlinde continued on with four other climbers. The team faced a number of harrowing moments before they finally made it to the top, making Gerlinde the first female to summit all of the world's tallest peaks without supplemental oxygen. The reading is based on the article *K2: Danger and Desire on the Savage Mountain*, written by Chip Brown for *National Geographic* magazine in 2012.

Online search terms: Gerlinde Kaltenbrunner, Danger and Desire on the Savage Mountain

 UNDERSTANDING THE READING
(pages 226–227)

A Summarizing

Students are asked to complete a summary of the passage.

- Have students work individually to complete the activity. Note that students can use words from the reading or synonyms with the same meaning.
- Check answers as a class. Discuss where students found the answers.

B Understanding Main Ideas

Students are asked to identify the ways the climbers handled fear, based on information in Paragraphs D–H.

- Have students work individually to complete the activity.
- Check answers as a class. Discuss where students found the answers.

C Sequencing

Students are asked to put the events of the climb in the correct order.

- Encourage students to try to put the events in order based on what they recall.
- Allow time for students to refer to the passage and check their answers.
- Have students form pairs to compare timelines.
- Check answers as a class.

D Inferring Meaning

Students find and underline the words in the passage. Then they use context to deduce the meaning of the words. Lastly, they match each word to its definition.

- Have students work individually to locate the words in the passage and deduce their meaning.
- Check answers as a class. Elicit example sentences for each word.

E Critical Thinking: Interpreting Figurative Language

The *Critical Thinking* box explains how to interpret and understand figurative language. Figurative language has a different meaning from the literal meaning of the words being used. It is especially common in literary writing, such as fiction, as well as in descriptive writing. However, some figurative language has also become colloquial and is used in everyday communication, too. For this exercise, students are asked to guess the meaning of figurative language, based on contextual clues.

- Have students work individually to complete the activity.
- Have them form pairs to compare their ideas.
- Check answers as a class.

F Critical Thinking: Reflecting

Students are asked to share their thoughts about mountaineering. Specifically, the exercise asks students to think more deeply about the final quote of the essay from Gerlinde, which explains why she thinks mountain climbing is worth it (important enough to do): "You see all this—I think everybody can understand why we do this."

- Allow students time to reread the quote at the end of Paragraph W.
- Have them work in pairs to discuss their answers. Tell students to give reasons for their opinions.
- Discuss as a class. After students share their thoughts, ask them to comment on whether or not they think the quote is an effective ending to the essay and why.

UNDERSTANDING THE READING

A **1.** 2011

2. K2

3. six (Explanation: Gerlinde, Ralf, Maxut, Vassiliy, Dariusz, Tommy)

4. camps

5. two

6. husband

7. weather / conditions / weather conditions

8. death zone

9. first woman

10. oxygen (Note: *extra* is a synonym for *supplemental*, which is why the answer is not *supplemental oxygen*)

B 1, 3, 4, 6 (See Paragraph E.)

C e, c, d, h, a, b, f ,g

D **1.** c

2. d

3. e

4. a

5. b

E Answers will vary. Possible answers:

1. The good weather was a happy surprise that was going to make their climbing possible that day.

2. To help readers visualize how small the human figures looked from where Ralf was standing.

3. Some of them probably lost their lives climbing K2 or other mountains, so it made her emotional when she made it to the summit.

F Answers will vary. Possible answers:

I don't think the risk is worth it because I don't believe a good view is worth dying for. There are many ways to see a great view without risking your life. / I think it's worth the risk. Mountain climbing tests a person's body and mind in a good way, and getting to the summit of a big mountain is the achievement of a lifetime.

DEVELOPING READING SKILLS
(page 228)

Reading Skill: Identifying Adverbial Phrases

The *Reading Skill* box explains the role of adverbial phrases in a sentence, and how to identify them. Adverbial phrases add information to a sentence, such as explaining when, why, where, or how something happens. Note that an adverbial phrase is not a clause, as it has no subject or verb. It can be easy to mix up an adverbial phrase that begins with *to* (infinitive of purpose) and an object that begins with *to*. If the phrase can be replaced with *in order to*, it is an adverbial phrase rather than an object. Point out that looking out for some key terms can help students quickly identify the adverbial phrase and its purpose: when (*during, by, in, on, then, later, before*, etc.), why (*to, for, from*), where (*in, on, above, below*, etc.), or how (*with, by*, etc.).

A Identifying Adverbial Phrases

Students are asked to underline adverbial phrases in the excerpts.

- Note that students should ignore the write-on lines in the right column for this exercise.
- Have students work individually to complete the exercise.
- Have them form pairs to compare answers.
- Check answers as a class.

B Identifying Adverbial Phrases

Students are asked to identify the role of each adverbial phrase in exercise **A**. What kind of information does each adverbial phrase provide?

- Have students work individually to complete the exercise.
- Have them form pairs to compare answers.
- Check answers as a class.

C Applying

Students are asked to find three more examples of adverbial phrases in the reading passage.

- Have students work in pairs to find the adverbial phrases.
- Explain that there may be more than three possible answers.
- Check answers as a class. Ask for volunteers to share the examples they found.

DEVELOPING READING SKILLS

A 1. <u>During the summer of 2011</u>, a team of climbers attempted to climb the world's second highest peak.

2. Their goal was to climb the North Ridge <u>on the Chinese side of the mountain</u>.

3. <u>To establish the route</u>, they had to cope with vertical rock walls, avalanches, …

4. If she succeeded, she would be the first woman in history to climb all of the world's tallest peaks <u>without supplemental oxygen</u>.

5. <u>On their first climb together</u>, Gerlinde and Ralf had made an agreement.

6. <u>Below them</u>, a terrifying void plunged to the glacier below.

7. But … the climbers made <u>painfully slow</u> progress.

8. They would rest <u>until morning</u>, then resume the push for the prize.

9. <u>With a surge of energy and hope</u>, she finally crawled onto the ridge.

10. <u>Fifteen minutes later</u>, Maxut and Vassiliy arrived, …

B 1. when   6. where
   2. where   7. how
   3. why   8. when
   4. how   9. how
   5. when   10. when

C Answers will vary. Possible answers:

Paragraph A: …Chinese side of the mountain, <u>without bottled oxygen or high-altitude porters</u>. (how)

Paragraph B: …who had previously reached the summit of K2 <u>from the Pakistani side</u>. (where)

Paragraph M: <u>By 1 p.m.</u> they had gained less than 180 meters. (when)

Paragraph R: <u>By mid-afternoon</u>, they reached the base of a ramp beneath the summit ridge. (when)

Video

VIEWING: SURVIVAL LESSONS
(pages 229–230)

Overview of the Video

The video presents two dangerous situations—a shark attack and an encounter with an elephant—and quizzes viewers on how to survive them. It also explains the best course of action for each scenario. The video is made up of two clips from the *Survival Guide* series that was featured on *National Geographic*.

Online search terms: surviving shark attacks, surviving elephant charges

BEFORE VIEWING

A Predicting

Students are presented with the quiz questions from the video and asked to predict the answers to them.

• Have students work in pairs to discuss what they think the answers may be.
• Have students check their answers later as they watch the video.

B Learning About the Topic

The chart provides students with some statistics on the number of human deaths caused by certain wild animals. Students then answer questions related to the information in the chart.

• Have students work individually to answer the questions.
• Elicit a class discussion. For question **2**, ask students to share their opinions and the reasons for them.

C Vocabulary in Context

This exercise introduces students to three vocabulary phrases used in the video. Students use context to deduce the meaning of the phrases.

• Have students work on the exercise individually.
• Ask students to form pairs and check their answers.
• Discuss answers as a class. Elicit example sentences for each phrase.

BEFORE VIEWING

A   Answers will vary. Correct answers:

1. b   **2.** c

B   Answers will vary. Possible answers:

1. Mosquitoes live in many different places and have the potential to spread diseases such as malaria to many people.

2. I'm most worried about snakes because I live near a forested area and sometimes I spot snakes in the grass.

C 1. tuck in (Note: Other common uses of this phrasal verb include *tuck in a shirt* and *tuck a child into bed.*)

2. stand your ground (Note: This phrase can also be used figuratively to refer to maintaining an opinion or viewpoint even when others disagree with you.)

3. catch up

WHILE VIEWING

A ▶ **Understanding Main Ideas**

Have students read the items before playing the video.

- Have them complete the task while the video is playing.
- Check answers as a class.

B ▶ **Understanding Details**

Have students read the questions and write any answers they recall from the first viewing before playing the video a second time.

- Play the video again. Have them complete the task while the video is playing.
- Check answers as a class. Ask students how the false statements should be edited to make them true. (See Answer Key.)

WHILE VIEWING

A   b

B 1. F (Explanation: *Of the more than 300 species of shark, only a small number are proven man-eaters.*)

2. F (Explanation: *Sharks may bite people out of hunger, but often as not, will bite out of simple curiosity.*)

3. T (Explanation: *Your best chance is to strike at its soft spots: its eyes, gills, and nose. Make the shark decide you're not worth the trouble.*)

4. T (Explanation: *It flares its ears and trumpets a warning.*)

5. T (Explanation: *Once you're engaged, you do not show your back to that elephant. You do not turn, you do not run…*)

6. T (Explanation: *He can easily, if he really wants to, he can catch up to you, and you just don't want to run away.*)

AFTER VIEWING

A Reacting to the Video

Students are asked to evaluate their guesses in exercise **A** of *Before Viewing*.

- Have students work in the same pairs that they did for exercise **A**.
- Allow them time to discuss their thoughts about the advice in the video.
- Discuss as a class. Were any students surprised by the advice in the video? Why?

B Reflecting

Students are asked to share any background knowledge they have on surviving encounters with wild animals.

- Have students work in pairs or in small groups to share their ideas.
- Discuss as a class. Ask volunteers to share what they discussed.
- If time permits, allow students to go online and do more research to check that their survival tips are accurate.

ANSWER KEY

AFTER VIEWING

A Answers will vary. Possible answer:

I didn't choose the same advice. I thought you were supposed to pretend to be dead. I never would have thought to attack a shark's eyes while it's biting me!

B Answers will vary. Possible answer:

I read that if you see a bear in the wild, you shouldn't run. You should speak in a calm voice and back away slowly.

Reading 2

30 MINS PREPARING TO READ *(page 231)*

A Building Vocabulary

The box contains ten key vocabulary words that appear in the reading passage. Students should first use a dictionary to check the definition of the words before completing the sentences.

- Have students complete the task individually.
- Check answers as a class. Elicit example sentences for each vocabulary item.

See Vocabulary Extension 10 in the Student Book for additional practice with adjectives ending in -ed and -ing.

B Using Vocabulary

Students should use the new vocabulary items while discussing the questions.

- Have students work in pairs to answer the questions. If necessary, provide prompts to support their discussion.
- Discuss as a class. Elicit responses from students.

C Brainstorming

Students are asked to reflect on how they deal with fear.
- Allow students time to note their answers individually.
- Have students form pairs to share their responses.
- Discuss as a class.

D Predicting

Students are asked to skim the reading and predict the topics in the passage.

- Allow students time to skim the reading and note their answers individually.
- Have students share their answers with a partner.
- Revisit this exercise after students have completed the reading.

ANSWER KEY

PREPARING TO READ

A			
1. version		**6.** separate	
2. alter		**7.** demonstrate	
3. crisis		**8.** consciously	
4. take over		**9.** assume	
5. instantly		**10.** determination	

B Answers will vary. Possible answers:

1. I think starting your own business requires a lot of determination. Success won't happen instantly, so you have to keep trying even after failing.

2. I think being calm is one of the best characteristics to have in a crisis.

3. Experiences that can alter a person's life include moving to a new country, having children, changing careers, etc.

C Answers will vary. Possible answer:

When I feel scared, I try to think about my dog because it helps calm me down. I imagine myself walking my dog in the park near my house. It's one of my favorite things to do, so thinking about it relaxes me.

D Answers will vary. Possible answer:

breathing techniques, survived a serious accident

🎧 **2.10** Have students read the passage individually, or play the audio and have students read along.

OVERVIEW OF THE READING

The passage discusses how breathing is a useful way to control fear response. It also presents a first-hand account of a photographer whose yoga and meditation training helped her survive a bus crash where she was severely injured. As she goes on to discuss the challenges of her recovery, we learn that she ultimately saw her traumatic experience as a gift that has led to her appreciating her life more. An interview with her can be found on *National Geographic Travel*.

Online search terms: Alison Wright, Traveler of the Year: Alison Wright

60 MINS UNDERSTANDING THE READING
(pages 235–236)

A Understanding Main Ideas

Students match each paragraph from the first part of the reading with its main idea.
- Have students work individually to complete the activity. Allow them time to refer to the reading as they do the exercise.
- Check answers as a class.

B Sequencing

Students put the events of Alison Wright's experience in the correct order.
- Have students work individually to complete the exercise.
- Check answers as a class.

C Understanding Details

Students answer questions about Alison Wright's story. Note that the questions are asking students to identify the conflict and resolution in the story.
- Have students work individually to answer the questions.
- Have them form pairs to check answers.

D Critical Thinking: Applying Ideas

Students identify the ideas about breathing and controlling our fear response that Alison Wright's story shows.
- Have students work in pairs.
- Check answers as a class. Discuss where in the reading students found the relevant information.

E Identifying Adverbial Phrases

Students practice the reading skill that they learned earlier in the unit. Students first underline the adverbial phrase and then identify its purpose.
- Have students work individually to complete the exercise.
- Check answers as a class.

F Critical Thinking: Interpreting Figurative Language

Students practice the critical thinking skill introduced in Reading 1.
- Have students work individually to note their ideas.
- Have students share their ideas in pairs.
- Discuss as a class.

G Critical Thinking: Synthesizing

Students are asked to compare the way Gerlinde Kaltenbrunner (from Reading 1) and Alison Wright dealt with their fear in highly stressful situations.
- Have students work individually to write their ideas.
- Have them form pairs to discuss ideas.
- If time permits, discuss as a class.

UNDERSTANDING THE READING

A **1.** B (Explanation: *One of the most surprising ways to control our fear response is breathing.*)

2. A (Explanation: *In fact, for most of history, we have assumed that there is a line separating our natural, basic instinct and our learned behavior.*)

3. D (Explanation: *One scientific study demonstrated how rhythmic breathing can actually alter the brain.*)

4. C (Explanation: *By consciously slowing down the breath, we can slow down the primal fear response that otherwise takes over.*)

5. E (Explanation: *With training, it may be possible to become better prepared for a life-or-death situation.*)

B (See Paragraphs G–J)

c, f, a, b, g, e, d

C **1.** She learned the techniques from meditation and yoga.

2. She had to rebuild muscles that had atrophied. / She had to rebuild abdominal muscles. / She had nightmares and PTSD.

3. She climbed Mt. Kilimanjaro. / She wrote a book. / She set up a charity and visited the people in Laos who helped her.

D 2, 4

E **1.** …to prepare FBI agents for crisis situations; why

2. By consciously slowing down the breath…; how

3. With training…; how

4. …to calm my breathing…; why

5. Every morning…; when

F Answers will vary. Possible answers:

1. To be "thrown into adversity," she unexpectedly had to deal with a crisis situation. To "come out on the other end," she was able to survive the difficult experience.

2. Her experience was a gift because it taught her to be grateful for everything in life.

G Answers will vary. Possible answers:

Both became calm in the face of fear, and both were able to survive as a result. / Both were able to use their training or experience to help them get through challenges. / Both never gave up in spite of the situations they faced.

Writing

OVERVIEW

In this section, students learn how to write a descriptive narrative essay. The lesson starts by reviewing the various past forms and when to use them. It then explains the elements and structure of a descriptive narrative. In the *Writing Task*, students apply these lessons by writing and revising a narrative about a true story of someone who survived danger or adversity. Students begin by researching online to find a story that interests them the most, before organizing the details in an outline. Students then draft their essays, improve their drafts, and correct common mistakes related to the use of verbs in the past form.

 EXPLORING WRITTEN ENGLISH
(pages 237–239)

A Noticing

Students identify the type of event described by each underlined verb in the sentences. This exercise is to be done before going over the information in the *Language for Writing* box.

- Explain that they should look at the descriptions (1–3) first before reading the sentences.
- Have students complete the task individually.
- Check answers as a class. Elicit more details. For example, what series of events happened in sentence **a**? (many unsuccessful attempts to climb Mount Everest)

Language for Writing: Using Past Forms for Narratives

The *Language for Writing* box reviews four forms of the past tense: simple past, past continuous (*was/were* + *-ing* form), past perfect (*had* + past participle), and past perfect continuous (*had been* + *-ing* form). Go over the examples and review the circumstances or reasons for using one form over another. Explain that the past tense is commonly used in a narrative to describe the events in the story. Point out that using a variety of verb forms is one way to keep your writing interesting and your readers engaged.

B Language for Writing

Students choose the correct past form of the verbs to complete the narrative paragraph.

- Have students work individually on the exercise.
- Have students form pairs to compare answers.
- Check answers as a class. If time permits, go over why each answer is a better choice than the other option. Elicit reasons from students, having them refer back to the *Language for Writing* box.

C Language for Writing

Students complete the sentences with the correct form of the past tense. Note that answers may vary. (See Answer Key.)

- Have students complete the activity individually.
- Have students compare answers in pairs.
- Check answers as a class.

Writing Skill: Writing a Descriptive Narrative Essay

The *Writing Skill* box introduces how to plan and organize a descriptive narrative essay. A narrative essay presents a personal story, and has a clear beginning, middle, and end. The introductory paragraph introduces the real character, sets the scene, and presents the thesis statement. In a narrative essay, a thesis statement often explains what the person learned or gained from the experience. In this case, how the person was able to overcome a crisis situation. The body of the essay recounts the details of what happened in sequential order. The concluding part of the essay talks about how the person found a resolution, and reached a positive outcome.

D Writing Skill

Students look back at Reading 2 and analyze the features of the first-person narrative account.

- Have students work in pairs to complete the activity.
- Allow them to refer to Reading 2 as they do the exercise.
- Check answers as a class.

E Writing Skill

Students choose the best thesis statement based on their analysis in exercise **D**.

- Have students work individually to complete the activity.
- Have students form pairs to compare answers.
- Check answers as a class. Ask students why this is the most suitable thesis statement.

EXPLORING WRITTEN ENGLISH

A 1. a

   2. c

   3. b

LANGUAGE FOR WRITING

B 1. had just completed

   2. arrived

   3. had received

   4. had been hiking

   5. had fallen

   6. was snowing

   7. was making

   8. sat

   9. got

  10. had learned

C 1. had climbed / had been climbing, decided (Note: The meaning of the sentence is slightly different depending on the verb form of *climb*. The past perfect can be used here to refer to a past state (climbing together). The past perfect continuous emphasizes the duration of an ongoing past event.)

   2. had attempted, succeeded

   3. was climbing / had been climbing, hit (Note: The meaning of the sentence is slightly different depending on the verb form of *climb*. The past continuous shows an ongoing past event that was interrupted. The past perfect continuous shows an ongoing past event that stopped after a certain point in the past.)

   4. had been waiting, got

WRITING SKILL

D 1. first person

   2. being in a bus crash

   3. a. Laos; b. back and ribs; c. control her breathing; d. an aid worker; e. seven hours

   4. After surviving and recovering from such a tragic event, she felt that it had made her more grateful about life. / Controlling her breathing kept her calm and alive until help arrived.

   5. Paragraph G: when, instantly

      Paragraph H: when, then

      Paragraph J: eventually, after, when, every morning

E   3

WRITING TASK *(page 240)*

A Brainstorming

Students brainstorm for the unit's essay by first thinking of possible dangerous situations people could face, e.g., being injured on a mountain. They then go online to find a person to write about and research details of that person's story. Read the *Goal* box aloud so students are familiar with the writing task before brainstorming. The aim of the essay is to write a descriptive narrative about someone who survived a dangerous situation or someone who overcame adversity.

- Encourage students to choose a person/story from their knowledge, if possible.
- Allow time for students to go online and find a story, if needed.
- Have students share their ideas with a partner. Tell partners to offer suggestions and feedback.

B Planning

Students complete the outline for their essays. Note that the details in the body paragraph will be composed of sequential events that happened during the crisis.

- Allow students time to look online for details for their story.
- Have students complete their outlines individually. Provide assistance as needed.

C First Draft

Have students write a first draft of their essays based on their outline.

- Allow students time to complete the task individually.
- Provide assistance as needed. Refrain from error correction at this point.

WRITING TASK

A   Answers will vary. Possible answers:

Michael Anereggen, mountain climber; was climbing Mount Temple in Banff, Canada

B   Answers will vary. Possible answers:

Introductory Paragraph

Survivor: Michael Andereggen

Setting: Mount Temple, Banff National Park

Conflict: fell 400 feet while mountain climbing

Thesis Statement: His situation seemed hopeless, but his calm decision making would help save his life.

Body Paragraphs

Topic Sentence 1 / Details: Andereggen woke up to find himself alone in the snow; injured, exhausted, no energy to climb

Topic Sentence 2 / Details: Andereggen saw that the rope he was climbing with was still wrapped around his upper body; rope had saved him from falling another 600 feet; his position was precarious; he realized he shouldn't move

Concluding Paragraph

Resolution: park employee rescued him

Summary Statement: Andereggen had learned that day that when your situation seems desperate, simply doing the next right thing can save your life.

REVISING PRACTICE *(page 241)*

The *Revising Practice* box contains an exercise that demonstrates several ways students can improve their first drafts.

- Allow students time to analyze the draft and complete the exercise. Note that this essay is an example of the writing task (a descriptive narrative about a survivor).
- Check answers as a class. Ask students to identify each change and explain how it makes the revised draft stronger.

D Revised Draft

Students should apply the revision techniques used in the *Revising Practice* box to their own drafts, where applicable.

- Explain to students that they will be using the questions as a guide for checking and improving their drafts.
- As a class, go over the questions carefully to make sure students understand them.
- Allow students time to revise their essays.

EDITING PRACTICE

The *Editing Practice* box trains students to spot and correct common errors related to using the past forms of verbs in a descriptive narrative.

- Allow students time to complete the exercise individually.
- Check answers as a class by asking students to read their corrected sentences aloud and explain the errors.

ANSWER KEY

REVISING PRACTICE

1. a, b, c
2. **d.** Sentence to cross out: Weather conditions on the mountain can change rapidly.
   e. He <u>realized</u> that he probably wouldn't survive another 24 hours in these conditions.
   f. Eventually, he <u>heard</u> someone ask, "Are you all right?"

EDITING PRACTICE

1. Wright <u>was</u> traveling in Laos when she was involved in an accident.
2. After the climbers had <u>set</u> up their camps, they began their ascent.
3. Ralf <u>explained</u> later that he was afraid he'd never see Gerlinde again.
4. She <u>had been planning</u> / <u>had planned</u> the climb for many years, and finally got the chance to do it in 2011.
5. Suddenly, Andereggen <u>fell</u> / <u>had fallen</u> 400 feet down the side of the mountain.

E Final Draft

Have students apply the skills taught in *Editing Practice* to their own revised drafts and check for any other errors.

- Allow students time to edit their drafts.
- Walk around and monitor students as they work. Provide assistance as needed.
- Collect their work once they have completed it.
- For the next class, show anonymous examples of good essays and common errors.

Ideas for ... EXPANSION

Have students work in groups of three to help review and edit each other's essays further. Ask each student to read another student's essay and do the following:

- Correct one error in grammar, spelling, etc.
- Give one compliment.
- Give one piece of feedback to help improve the essay.

Allow students time to read each other's essays, take notes, and discuss their feedback.

 10 MINS

UNIT REVIEW

Students can work in groups on this recap of the unit. For question **1**, encourage students to use the target vocabulary words when appropriate. For questions **2** and **3**, encourage them to check the relevant pages of the unit for answers.

- Allow students time to answer the questions in groups.
- Ask each group to present its answer for question **1**.

VIDEO TRANSCRIPTS

UNIT 1 Elephant Orphans

Narrator It's daybreak at The David Sheldrick Wildlife Trust on the edge of Nairobi's National Park. Orphaned elephants and their human caretakers wake up to a beautiful African morning.

Little Shimba came here last September when he was only six weeks old. He was found near his dead mother in the Tsavo National Park. Ten-month-old Chuyla was found stuck in a water hole. She had been orphaned days earlier when her mother was killed by poachers. Many of the orphans here had mothers killed by poachers.

In all, more than 100 orphaned elephants have been saved by The David Sheldrick Wildlife Trust. Eighty of these elephants have survived. And it's not as easy as it seems. Elephant babies stay with their mothers for years. The fat content in the milk of nursing mother elephants varies depending on the baby's age.

Daphne Sheldrick founded The David Sheldrick Wildlife Trust in 1977, in memory of her husband. It took her more than two decades to find the right milk formula—and care—needed to keep orphaned elephants alive.

Daphne Sheldrick I discovered how to raise an infant African elephant just through trial and error. We found that giving them cow's milk killed them straight away. And then baby milk started coming on to the market for cow's-milk-sensitive human children.

Narrator An infant elephant consumes 24 pints of specially formulated milk every 24 hours. When the elephant is six months old, it consumes even more milk. At this point, dried coconut and cooked oatmeal porridge are added to the milk formula. Besides large amounts of food, growing elephants also need a lot of interaction with caregivers. Elephants are social creatures, so the keepers are by their sides 24 hours a day—just as a mother elephant would stay close to her own children.

A blanket mimics maternal warmth when caregivers feed the elephants. The babies hang their trunks on it, just as they would lay them across their own mother's belly. And like human children, young elephants like to play. Some experts believe that elephants have a complex social and emotional life similar to humans.

Edwin Lusichi The care we're giving them is the same as we give to human babies. We feed them, we nurse them, we sleep with them in the same house. We lie down sometimes on the mattresses. We cover them with the blankets just like we do to our human babies. And they behave like human babies: What you tell them not to do is what they want to do. And where you want them not to go is where they want to go.

Narrator Edwin Lusichi has been at The Trust since 1999. There are 51 keepers here in all. Their task is to care for the elephants until they leave and join other elephants in the wild. The reintroduction back to the wild can take up to 10 years. Some elephants have gone on to successfully reproduce.

Thirty years ago, it's estimated that about three million elephants roamed through Africa. Today, there are only about 250,000 left. The great beasts were slaughtered for their ivory tusks and for meat. Much of their habitat has been destroyed by human development. These dangers continue to this day.

After a long day, the orphans are ready for some much-needed rest. The littlest elephants go to bed with a caring member of their adoptive family. Like human babies, they will wake periodically during the night in search of comfort and food. Adolescents sleep together.

Shimba takes a little snack before bedtime. These orphans are all safe here—for the time being. The Trust hopes these young animals will have a bright future under the African sky.

UNIT 2 Secrets in the Ice

Albert Zink My name is Albert Zink. I'm the head of the Institute for Mummies and the Iceman here at the European Academy in Bolzano, Italy. I'm responsible for the research on the Iceman, a 5,300-year-old mummy.

Narrator In 1991, the Iceman's body was discovered in the Ötztal Alps—an area on the border of Austria and Italy. Through an examination of the body, researchers found that the Iceman was killed by an arrow shot.

Albert Zink It's such an interesting story. It's a crime story. And for sure we want to know about how he died and why he died. And because it's also such a spectacular finding, this mummy. Such an old mummy. It's the only one we have here in this region of such a high age.

Man Do you think there could be more mummies in this area?

Albert Zink Maybe. Maybe. I think there could be some. At least some evidence from other people. Maybe also just some other arrows. Maybe it was not just one shot. Or maybe there were more people, and we are losing some things or leaving some equipment here.

I think the Iceman is so special because on the one hand, he's perfectly preserved and he really gives us unique insights into this time that we don't know so much about.

He contains a lot of information also on different diseases. He had some genetic predisposition for coronary heart diseases. And this is a disease what we always believed is a modern day disease. I think we can learn a lot if we study these mummies and understand how … what role plays the genes and what role plays the nutrition. This could help to find new ways to avoid the diseases or to better also deal with these diseases. In the end, the Iceman is one of our ancestors, and it's very interesting to understand also the past and where we came from. And how they already were able to adapt to the environment, how they managed to live, and without all these modern technologies we have and so on. You can really still feel somehow that this person was alive 5,000 years ago.

Narrator Albert Zink thinks that there could be more secrets up in the mountains. He believes that a deeper investigation might reveal more clues about the Iceman's death, such as who killed him and why, and whether there were other people with him. With further study, scientists hope that they can uncover what truly happened to the Iceman of the Alps.

UNIT 3 Farming Underground

Dring We are in southwest London. Clapham North Station is about 100 yards in that direction. We are in a tunnel system that was built during the Second World War, and we are 100 feet under London.

Narrator These tunnels were left empty after World War II, but entrepreneurs Steven Dring and Richard Ballard have plans for this underground space: They want to build a carbon-neutral farm.

Dring And that's what you see behind us, glowing pink. And it is a hydroponic farm that is powered by LEDs and those LEDs are all … all the energy for the LEDs are powered by renewable energy.

Narrator A lot of food today is imported from overseas, but by building a farm in the middle of the city, Dring and Ballard hope they can encourage people to eat locally grown food and learn more about where their food comes from.

Dring We've still got kids in the U.K. who think that spaghetti is grown on trees. This is a problem that we've got in terms of that disconnect from food.

We are trying to cut down on those food miles, bring food closer to the people that consume it.

If you project into the future—10, 20, 30 years—and how people will be dining then, people will become more and more and more aware of the environment around us.

In London, for example, we're going to have an additional two million people in the next 10 years, and we need to provide for that. So, it's about making sure that we have a food source that's from a new environment.

And so we got one bench, but when we populate it—the whole of the tunnel—we'll have a bench on the floor, bench halfway up, and a bench up here as well, so we'll be growing that. That's the multilayered system, and that would be each side of this tunnel, so it's about utilizing all of the space that we've got down here.

UNIT 4 Hurricanes

Violent winds, driving rain, killer waves. These are the hallmarks of a hurricane. Also called cyclones or typhoons, hurricanes are giant storms that form in the world's tropical seas. An average hurricane releases as much energy in a day as the explosion of half a million small atomic bombs.

Hurricanes form in the summer and fall, when the sun heats vast stretches of tropical ocean to over 82 degrees. Warm, moist air rises over these hot spots, creating thunderstorms. Upper level winds and surface winds then come together, forming a circular pattern of clouds known as a tropical depression. When the winds exceed 39 miles per hour, a tropical storm has developed. When the winds reach 74 miles per hour, a hurricane is officially born.

Inside the storm, bands of rain up to 300 miles long meet in the eyewall, the most violent section. Here, winds of up to 200 miles per hour spiral upward. Within the center of the hurricane, dry air blowing downward creates a strangely calm area called the eye. Fully formed, a hurricane may stretch over 500 miles in diameter—a storm nearly the size of Texas—and reach a height of 9 miles.

Most of these storms spin out over the open sea. But in an average year, two or three will strike the mainland of North America. When they do, the damage can be catastrophic. Most dangerous is the storm surge, a wall of water that sweeps across the coastline where a hurricane makes landfall.

About 45,000 people were killed by hurricanes in the 20th century, including some 15,000 in the United States. Hurricanes are also costly in dollars. In 1992, Hurricane Andrew caused more than 25 billion dollars' worth of damage. Since then, even more severe hurricanes have hit North America, including Hurricane Katrina in 2005 and Hurricanes Harvey, Irma, and Maria in 2017.

Scientists are searching for better ways to predict the path of a hurricane. Special planes called "hurricane hunters" fly directly into these monster storms and drop sensors to measure wind speed, temperature, and air pressure— providing vital clues to the hurricane's direction.

New 3-D models are also helping scientists understand this awesome force of nature, and provide quicker and more accurate warnings to anyone unlucky enough to be caught in its path.

UNIT 5 Galápagos Tourism

Narrator The Galápagos is a collection of 13 main islands in the Pacific Ocean. They are a thousand kilometers—or six hundred miles—from the coast of Ecuador in South America. The Galápagos is famous for the animal species that live here. Because the islands are isolated, animals evolved into unique species that do not exist anywhere else in the world.

But another species is invading these tropical islands— humans. They've been living here for more than a century. But in the past few decades, tourism has increased dramatically. And workers from Ecuador have come, too, to open businesses and provide services for the tourists. Some estimate the local population on the islands has increased by as much as 300 percent.

Lauren Spurrier In the 1980s, there was a local population of about 3,000 people living here on the islands, and today, we have a local population of more than 25,000 people.

Narrator Tourism brings much-needed revenue. But all these people generate pollution through vehicle emissions and energy consumption. And like almost all humans, they create trash. Environmentalists worry that tourism is having a negative impact on the islands' original inhabitants—the animals.

Recently, an oil tanker that was trying to deliver fuel to the Galápagos crashed. The oil spill that resulted from the crash eventually killed an estimated 60 percent of nearby iguanas. Researchers now say even a small amount of pollution can harm the islands' famous animal species.

Fortunately, the oil spill turned out to be a wake-up call. Now, with a series of ambitious projects, environmentalists and corporations are working together with the Ecuadorian government to minimize human impact. The goal is to end the use of fossil fuels on the Galápagos in the next decade, and to use only renewable, nonpolluting energy.

The goal is to make the islands "green." For example, these modern oil tanks replace rusty older ones that were about to fall into the sea. Contaminants in the fuel are removed to reduce pollution. An ultra-modern gas station has barriers to contain leaks. There's an ambitious plan to convert boat engines to cleaner and more efficient engines. And to replace cars on the islands with low-emissions vehicles.

A World Wildlife Fund recycling campaign is teaching islanders about the importance of preserving the natural beauty of their islands. For example, Lourdes Peñaherrera and her family have won a World Wildlife Fund award for reducing the amount of waste they produce.

Lourdes Penaherrera (translated) "Not only us, but the whole community has to recycle," she says. "It's to protect the environment. Almost everybody in our neighborhood does it now."

Narrator Environmentalists say humans will continue to have an impact on the Galápagos, but local cooperation, combined with the help of international environmental organizations, such as the World Wildlife Fund, may help to control the impact. There once were no people on these isolated islands, but now the world has arrived. Instead of ruining the Galápagos Islands, perhaps with a united effort, they will save them.

UNIT 6 Painting with Numbers

Jer Thorp We first started hearing about data visualization in the late 1800s, early 1900s, with graphics like this. This is Florence Nightingale's graphic showing the casualty count of soldiers, and her point was that soldiers were dying more of disease than they were dying on the battlefield. At the same time, John Snow produced this famous graphic which plotted the incidence of cholera in a certain area of London. And from this graphic, he was able to discover what the source of that cholera epidemic was—in this case, it was a single well.

[…] So, I'd suggest there are two reasons why we visualize data. To reduce things, to make them simpler, and to reveal things, to show us things that we have never seen before.

Narrator In 2009, Thorp created this infographic which he calls "Just Landed." First, he gathered data on Twitter. He looked for tweets like "I've just landed in Hawaii" or "I've just landed in New York." Then, he looked for information on users' profiles to find out where they were from. The final result was a visual representation of world travel—just by listening to people on Twitter.

Infographics help us see the world in a different way. They can also help us understand complex information. This is a scientific report published by the Kepler project team in 2011, describing the search for exoplanets—planets outside of our solar system. The paper contains a lot of detailed information and charts, but Thorp wondered, "Is there a more interesting way to present this information?"

Jer Thorp So, I thought, "How could I understand this system a little bit better?" So, I sat down for about a day, and I created a visualization of that data.

Narrator Thorp placed all of the exoplanets that had been discovered by Kepler as if they were circling a single star. He also represented each exoplanet using color and size. In this way, he was able to better understand the exoplanets—such as their distance from their star, their size, and how hot they are.

By reorganizing the data, Thorp shows how visualization can help us see and think about things from different angles. He feels the Kepler project is one of the best examples of his strategy for designing graphics.

Jer Thorp And this strategy—it's a two-word strategy—it's called "Ooh/Aah." And that means, the first thing that I want people to do is I want them to say "Ooh" when they see the visualization, but that "ooh" is useless unless there's an "aah." I want that learned moment that comes from really being able to discover something that you didn't understand before.

Narrator According to Thorp, if there's too much "ooh," then the infographic may look impressive, but may not actually have enough information. On the other hand, an infographic with too much "aah" may be overly detailed and not very engaging. So the next time you look at an infographic, consider this: is there a good balance of "ooh" and "aah"?

UNIT 7 The Snow Guardian

Narrator Have you ever wondered if you watched the snow long enough, what stories it might tell? There is someone who has done it. His name is billy barr.

billy barr I spell it, small b-i-l-l-y, small b-a-r-r.

Narrator Some people call him the snow guardian. He lives in a cabin out in the woods.

billy barr Picture this: it's a snowy day, it's dark and cold, and you make a fire and you're sitting by the fire, and you're reading with a cup of tea, and it goes on for nine months.

Narrator billy lives alone in this house he helped build. Here he grows his garden, has an impressive hat collection, loves cricket, and dreams of Bollywood. Every couple of weeks, he skis back into the nearest town for supplies. He's been doing this for more than 40 winters. But billy does a little more than just read and drink tea. For those 40 winters, billy has kept a meticulous record of snow in his little part of the world.

billy barr Okay … February 26th, 1978, ten and a half inches of snow that day. January 28th, minus eleven and a half. April 28th, 1980, I was forty-one. Oh, that sounds nice. 1997, one-half inch knee snow, a weasel was roaming around inside the shack, and the birds were back.

I lived in a 8-by-10 foot old shack. I had no electricity, no water, and I had nothing, and I was just there all day. The main thing I interacted with was the weather and the animals. So I started recording things just because it was something to do. I had nothing to prove, no goals, no anything. So, actually, the researchers, the lab, wanted to look at it. And then once he started looking at it scientifically, then, all of a sudden, like, these decades worth of data were being used for more than my own curiosity.

Narrator billy has done this every day, twice a day, all winter long.

billy barr I keep going until the snow is gone. If it snowed, I record that no matter when.

The trend I see is that we're getting a permanent snowpack later, and we get to bare ground sooner. We'll have years where there was a lot of snow on the ground, and then we lost snow sooner than years that had a lot less snow, just because it's a lot warmer now.

Narrator In a normal winter, you'd expect to have 4 to 5 record high temperatures. Last year, billy recorded 36.

billy barr Not only is it a lot warmer, we're getting a lot of dust blowing in. Soon as you get dust on the snow, it melts like that. You're talking about the snowpack, the water supply for most of the southwest. I'm not real hopeful, just because I don't know how you reverse something like that.

UNIT 8 Healthcare Innovator

Infectious diseases take a lot of lives. That's why we need technologies that could monitor, diagnose, and mitigate those diseases better, especially in developing countries. My name is Aydogan Ozcan. I'm an engineer and a National Geographic Emerging Explorer.

What I do is engineering solutions for global health challenges that leverage existing digital components, like cell phones, by bringing new technologies running on cell phones, for instance, to diagnose diseases. And what is quite timely about this vision is that we have close to six billion cell phone subscribers today, and more than 70 percent of these cell phones are actually being used in developing parts of the world.

Some of the technologies that we developed in our research lab that literally converts the cell phone itself into a platform that we can track, diagnose, monitor diseases globally. What we have here is an attachment to the back of the camera of the phone. And then there's an application—smart application—running on the cell phone, which will essentially process a rapid diagnostic test that you insert.

So the healthcare worker will be inserting it into the back as shown here, and then there is a smart application running on the phone where you start a new test. And then there's a menu. We inserted here a malaria diagnostic test, so you click on "Malaria," and what you see here is actually an image of the diagnostic test.

To understand that, all the user has to do is click on this image, and then now it's captured that image and processed it in real time to tell us that it was a valid test and the result was positive. Then the results can be uploaded to a central server, so that the policy makers or the healthcare workers can screen a region so that they

can understand the cause-effect relationships of some of the outcomes of different diseases that they are mitigating.

UNIT 9 Enduring Voices

Narrator They've been traveling the world, searching for words and ideas at risk of being lost forever. David Harrison and Greg Anderson—linguists with the Living Tongues Institute—and photographer Chris Rainier of the National Geographic Society were recently in northern Australia, where they interviewed a man who may be the last speaker of his language.

Man That's like "my father."

Greg Anderson My father.

Narrator There are seven thousand known languages in the world, but more than half of these languages are expected to die out in the coming decades. And when a language disappears, so does valuable information. That's why Harrison, Anderson, and Rainier helped create National Geographic's Enduring Voices Project.

Chris Rainier Every two weeks around the planet, a language disappears. Completely disappears forever and ever. So what we're doing with the Enduring Voices Project is really kind of trying to bring awareness to this whole issue of language loss around the planet.

Narrator After Australia, the team continues the search for disappearing languages. This time, they are in the extreme northeast of India, a remote area bordering Bhutan, Myanmar, and China. It's considered a language "hot spot"—a region with great linguistic diversity and great risk of linguistic extinction.

Most of these local languages have never been written down. Many of them have never been recorded. This time, the researchers hope to collect more information on them than ever before.

The team arrives in a large village called Hong. After speaking to several villagers, it seems that the local Apatani language is widely spoken among the older generation. But the survival of a language, like many aspects of culture, depends on young people.

David Harrison It's very easy in these communities to find young people who are speaking English and Hindi and not speaking the traditional languages. They are neglecting them, they're perhaps even abandoning them.

Narrator The team meets a young man named Vijay who speaks English and Apatani. Vijay invites them into his home. Here, with the help from Indian scholar Dr. Ganesh Murmu, the researchers record the basics of the local language.

Dr. Murmu How do you count one, two, three …

Narrator Each member of the family contributes some more valuable words. In addition to conducting their own research, the team trains local people to use special language technology kits. Each kit contains a laptop computer, digital video and still cameras, and basic digital recorders. The goal is to help communities document the last speakers of old languages, using new technologies. Apatani is a good example of the issue of language extinction.

David Harrison Not only are these languages very small, with just a few thousand speakers in some cases, but their numbers may be decreasing as people shift over to global languages.

Narrator The Enduring Voices team must leave Hong. But they leave behind the technology kits so that the community can continue to preserve this vital part of their heritage.

They hope the kits will help inspire younger people to take an interest in the words of their elders, perhaps encouraging them to keep a language alive by speaking it themselves. But no matter what happens, the recordings they make will ensure that, even if the last speakers of a native language die, we will still be able to hear them.

UNIT 10 Survival Lessons

Narrator Few animals inspire more fear than sharks. But out of the millions of people worldwide who swim in the ocean each year, less than a hundred are attacked. Of the more than 300 species of shark, only a small number are proven man-eaters. The most dangerous are tiger sharks, bull sharks, and great whites. A bite from them can literally cost life and limb.

Sharks may bite people out of hunger, but often as not, will bite out of simple curiosity. They'll gladly sample anything unusual bobbing in the water, like a person, just to see what it tastes like. So knowing how to respond can mean the difference between life and death.

If a shark attacks, should you … A. splash violently? B. go for the eyes? Or C. play dead?

The correct answer is B: go for the eyes. Splashing violently only attracts more sharks toward you. Playing dead leads to being dead. A limp body tells the shark it's time to tuck in for a big meal.

Your best chance is to strike at its soft spots: its eyes, gills, and nose. Make the shark decide you're not worth the trouble. And while it's deciding, get to shore as fast as you can. And that's how you survive a shark attack.

In the African rain forests of Congo, biologist Mike Fay runs into a three-ton surprise. The elephant seems more curious than alarmed—until it starts to lumber towards Mike.

It flares its ears and trumpets a warning. If it charges Mike, he could easily be crushed. So, what's the best way to avoid its dangerous charge? Should he … A. run between its legs? B. turn and run away? Or C. scream and yell? According to Mike Fay, the correct answer is C: scream and yell.

Mike Fay Once you're engaged, you do not show your back to that elephant. You do not turn, you do not run, 'cause if you do, he will chase you.

They're very fast, they're stealthy. He can easily, if he really wants to, he can catch up to you, and you just don't want to run away.

The probability of getting killed is much lower if you stand your ground than if you run. And yell—louder and louder and louder.

I don't know who was more nervous—me or her.

GRAPHIC ORGANIZERS

Unit 1 Social Relationships

Complete the chart as you read *Gender in the Wild*.

ANIMAL SPECIES	COUNTRY OF STUDY	BEHAVIOR OBSERVED IN FEMALES	BEHAVIOR OBSERVED IN MALES
Elephants 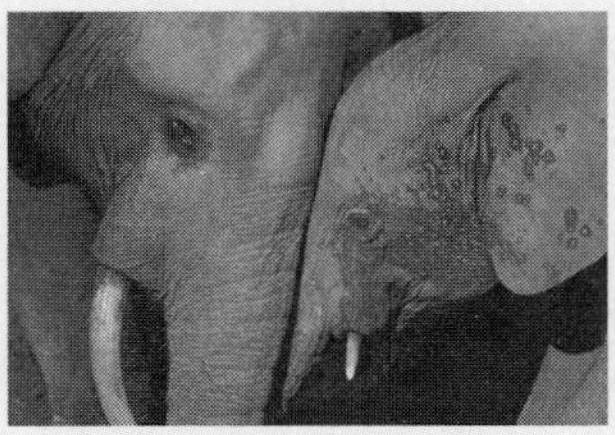		*Female elephants cooperate to raise their young.*	
Geladas 			
Chimps 			

Unit 2 Science and Investigation

Complete the summary diagram as you read *King Tut's Family Secrets*.

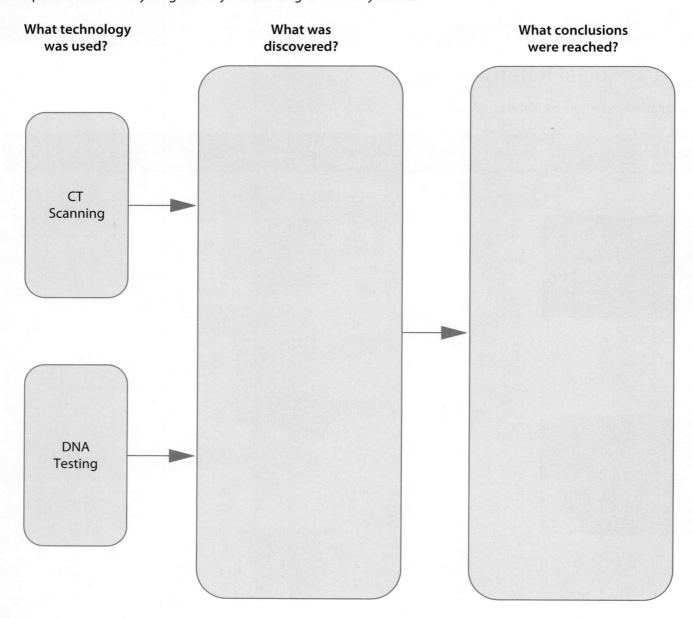

What technology was used?

CT Scanning

DNA Testing

What was discovered?

What conclusions were reached?

Unit 3 City Solutions

Read the three questions below. Then complete the concept map as you read *Living on an Urban Planet*.

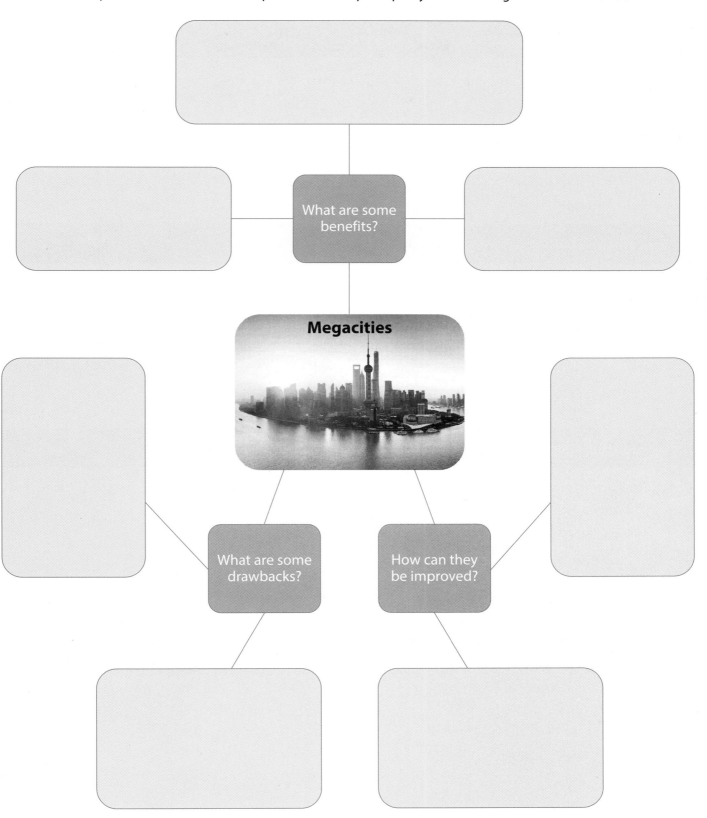

Megacities

What are some benefits?

What are some drawbacks?

How can they be improved?

Unit 4 Danger Zones

Complete the notes as you read *Yellowstone's Smoking Bomb*.

A. What are some characteristics of supervolcanoes?

B. How are supervolcanoes formed?

C. What are the effects of a super-eruption?

D. Why is it difficult to predict an eruption?

Unit 5 The Travel Business

Complete the chart as you read *Geotourism in Action*.

	ECOLODGE TOURISM IN ECUADOR	ADVENTURE TREKKING IN NEPAL	CULTURAL TOURS IN AUSTRALIA
What is it?			
How does it help the community?			
How does it help the environment?			
Any other benefits?			

Unit 6 Information Design

Complete the notes as you read *The Rise of Visual Data*.

A. Where visual data can be found

B. Advantages of good visual data

C. Possible problems of visual data

D. Predictions for the future of visual data

Unit 7 Global Challenges

Complete the chart as you read *A Need for Change*. For the supporting evidence, include relevant data from the figures in the passage where appropriate.

FACT	MAIN IDEA	SUPPORTING EVIDENCE
1. The world is warming.		
2. It's because of us.		
3. We're sure.		
4. Ice is melting fast.		
5. Weather is getting intense.		
6. Wildlife is already hurting.		
7. We can do something about it.		

Unit 8 Medical Innovations

Complete the summary diagram as you read *Medical Frontiers*.

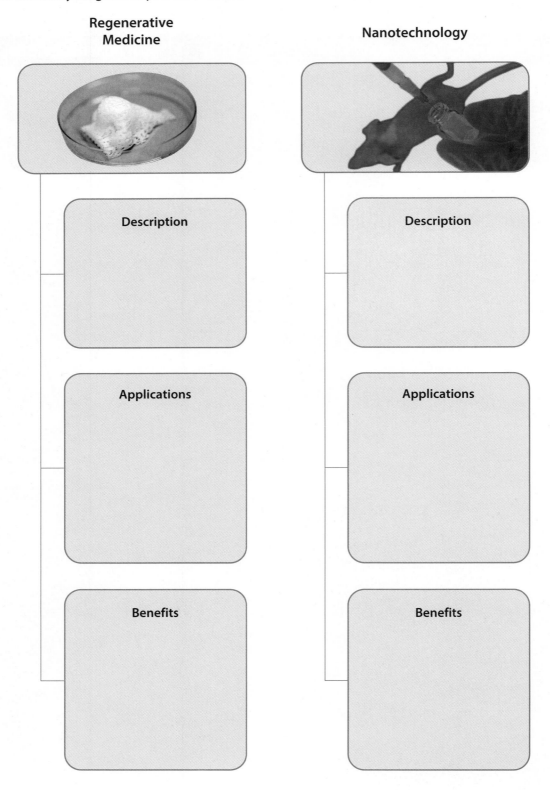

Regenerative
Medicine

Nanotechnology

Description

Description

Applications

Applications

Benefits

Benefits

Unit 9 World Languages

Complete the concept map as you read *Vanishing Voices*.

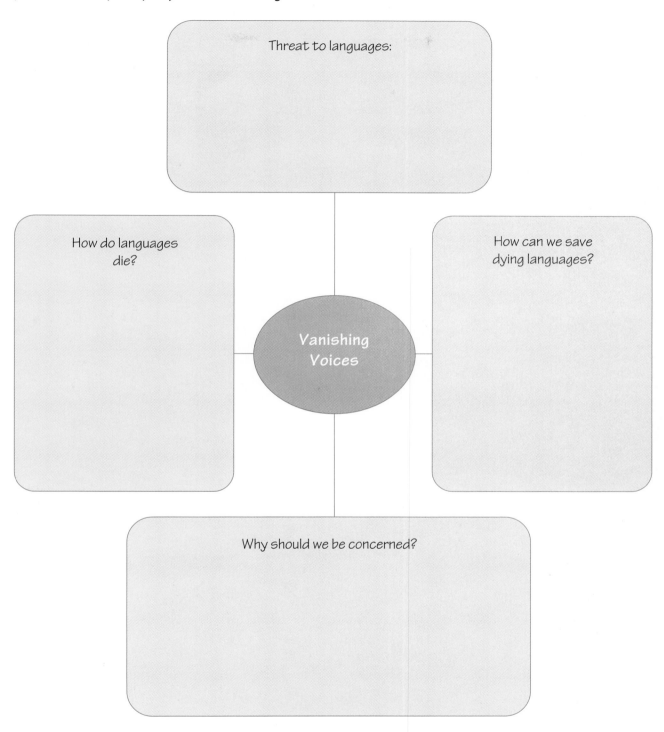

Threat to languages:

How do languages die?

How can we save dying languages?

Vanishing Voices

Why should we be concerned?

Unit 10 Survival Instinct

Complete the timeline of events in Alison Wright's life since January 2000. Use information from Reading 2: *A Survivor's Story*.

JANUARY 2000	
2004	
2005 AND AFTER	